High Risk and High Stakes

Recent Titles in
Contributions in Sociology

HIGH RISK
AND
HIGH STAKES

Health Professionals, Politics, and Policy

EARL WYSONG

Foreword by Robert Perrucci

Contributions in Sociology, Number 100

GREENWOOD PRESS
Westport, Connecticut • London

363.11
W99h

Library of Congress Cataloging-in-Publication Data

Wysong, Earl.
   High risk and high stakes : health professionals, politics, and
policy / Earl Wysong ; foreword by Robert Perrucci.
     p.   cm.—(Contributions in sociology, ISSN 0084-9278 ; no.
100)
   Includes bibliographical references (p.) and index.
   ISBN 0-313-28475-X (alk. paper)
   1. Medical policy—United States. 2. Occupational diseases—Law
and legislation—United States. 3. Industrial hygiene—Law and
legislation—United States. 4. Medicine—United States—Societies,
etc. I. Title. II. Series.
RA395.A3W93   1992
363.11'0973—dc20   91-47158

British Library Cataloguing in Publication Data is available.

Library of Congress Catalog Card Number: 91-47158
ISBN: 0-313-28475-X
ISSN: 0084-9278

First published in 1992

Greenwood Press, 88 Post Road West, Westport, CT 06881
An imprint of Greenwood Publishing Group, Inc.

Printed in the United States of America

The paper used in this book complies with the
Permanent Paper Standard issued by the National
Information Standards Organization (Z39.48-1984).

10 9 8 7 6 5 4 3 2 1

TP

CONTENTS

FOREWORD

It is difficult to understand the workings of contemporary industrial society without considering organizations as central elements or building blocks of the structure of modern society. A large body of scholarly research has provided rich documentation of the scope and centrality of organizations in virtually all areas of human activity and at all stages in the life cycle. Organizations are repositories of resources that are used to motivate and mobilize social action--money, jobs, information, votes, violence, moral authority--and there is continuous competition among groups interested in withholding or committing organizational resources for some activity.

It is known that organizations do not always act in isolation. They often pool their resources along industry lines or political interests to form trade associations and political action committees in order to advance individual and collective interests. The possibilities of collective action by organizations has stimulated study of interorganizational networks and the ways in which they can act in concert. Sometimes collective action may be directed by intraindustry competition to obtain advantage in the market place, and sometimes it is directed by an interest in shaping public policy.

This book makes the usually abstract notions of organizational power, interests, and network linkages comprehensible in its examination of the struggle over national legislation on occupational health policy. Wysong provides in-depth analysis of the activities undertaken by seven health and safety professional associations to support or defeat the High Risk Occupational Disease Notification and Prevention Act. Two very significant contributions of this book should be emphasized.

Wysong's research shatters the artificial division between the profit and nonprofit sectors. This rare glimpse into the operation of health professional's *organizations* reveals that political and economic interests shape the way in which professional associations become involved in the formation of health policy. This is a far cry from the view of professional associations as bodies of detached, objective experts who combine their knowledge and ethical codes to advise policy makers about the implications of alternative courses of action.

Using extensive archival data and interviews with senior personnel in professional associations, congressional subcommittees, and business and labor groups, Wysong informs about how "insiders" view each other and develop their position on the High Risk legislation. The examination of intraassociation politics is absorbing and calls to mind the incisive observation by Arthur Stinchcombe that the units in network analysis are organizations, and "are themselves networks of relations among positions, which is why they can act." Wysong helps us to see what goes on in the "nodes" of a network of professional associations by distinguishing between those organizations that speak with one voice on policy issues and those with competing internal interests that produce shifting and contradictory positions on policy issues. For example, it is only through the examination of the American Medical Association's internal networks that we are able to understand why the AMA staff members were supporters of the High Risk legislation while officers and trustees were opposed. While other analysts would accept the AMA's endorsement of the High Risk legislation as support for the bill, Wysong's examination of the competing interests of staff members, leader networks, membership, and external constituencies reveals the strength of opposition to the legislation.

Aside from specific contributions to organizational analysis, *High Risk and High Stakes* is an exemplary model of how sociological research should be conducted. Research is not simply applying a set of specific techniques to achieve desired results. It is a process which emphasizes the interplay of theory and method, so that concepts and ideas are reexamined and reformulated whenever unexpected findings are confronted. Wysong sometimes tells us more than we may want to know about his dilemmas and choices at various points in the research process, but we never feel left out. The author's intellectual and personal engagement with the politics of health policy is communicated throughout this work and makes this carefully researched study a pleasure to read.

Robert Perrucci

PREFACE

A recent report in the *American Journal of Public Health* on toxic exposures and community tensions advised health professionals that to be effective in such circumstances they must "avoid identification with extraneous agendas" (Leviton et al. 1991:692). The authors make the point that the credibility and efficacious involvement of health professionals in dealing with public health problems related to toxic exposures can be compromised if members of adversely affected groups perceive health scientists as having links to materially interested parties. This advice addresses a growing recognition that workers, consumers, and community members are less and less willing to assume health professionals automatically occupy a position of neutrality or that they can be routinely trusted to provide disinterested scientific expertise as a means of resolving controversial health policy issues.

As the public has grown more skeptical of the value-neutral claims of health professionals, "new class" theorists and researchers in sociology have also begun to look more closely at the question of the interests and allegiances of professionals where matters of public policy and reform are concerned (Brint 1984; Lamont 1987; McAdams 1987; Macy 1988). Although new class theory has been more vague than coherent concerning professionals' beliefs and behaviors on policy issues, it has raised important questions about the role of professionals in the policy reform process. Rather than trying to resolve the question of which "side" professionals are on in public policy disputes, the general objective of this book is to explore the issue of how and why organizations of health and safety professionals participate in the policy reform process.

THE HIGH RISK LEGISLATION
AND PROFESSIONAL SOCIETIES

From 1985 to 1988 Congress considered and nearly passed the "High Risk Occupational Disease Notification and Prevention Act." In its most basic form the High Risk legislation mandated individual notification of workers whose workplace exposures substantially increased their risks for developing job-related diseases. Moreover, most versions of the legislation also required medical monitoring of high risk workers to facilitate early disease detection, treatment, and job transfers (U.S. Congress: House, 1985; 1987a; Senate 1987a; 1987b). This legislation was the first major occupational health policy reform effort in over fifteen years. It ignited a firestorm of controversy and intense lobbying which involved not only business and labor groups but also several professional societies as well.

The unique and controversial features of the High Risk bills afford us a once-in-a-generation opportunity to explore the political dynamics of the policy process in the area of occupational health legislation and the role of professional societies in that process. The seven associations whose policy involvement we focus upon are: (1) American Association of Occupational Health Nurses (AAOHN), (2) American Conference of Governmental Industrial Hygienists (ACGIH), (3) American Industrial Hygiene Association (AIHA), (4) American Medical Association (AMA), (5) American Occupational Medical Association (AOMA), (6) American Public Health Association (APHA), (7) American Society of Safety Engineers (ASSE).

OBJECTIVES OF THE BOOK

The specific objectives of the book are framed around answers to a series of interrelated questions regarding the High Risk legislation and the participation of the seven professional associations in its development:

1. Why did the High Risk legislation emerge as a major policy issue in the mid-1980s, and how were the conflicting interests of organized labor and business involved in structuring the organizational divisions/alignments, and compromises/confrontations related to the legislation during the 1985-88 period?
2. Throughout 1985-88, what basic policy positions (i.e., support or opposition) were adopted by each of the seven associations regarding the High Risk legislation?

3. What types and levels of organizational resources did the professional societies commit to their basic policy decisions concerning the
legislation?
4. On the basis of theoretical considerations, what interorganizational
linkages are most relevant to identifying, understanding, and explain-
ing the associations' decision-making processes, policies, and resource
commitment-decisions?
5. Finally, within the context of the period were there events and/or
circumstances which either separately or in conjunction with organizational and/or interorganizational factors influenced the policy and
resource commitment decisions of the seven organizations?

As a result of addressing these specific questions, more general issues
related to the role of the professions in social change can also be explored.
These include the case for expanding the traditional view of health policy into
a multidimensional concept, efforts to clarify the influence of ethics and
interests upon the organizational behavior of professional societies, and finally,
an assessment of whether, or the extent to which, professionals act as a force
for social reform.

A NOTE ON STYLE

Although this book is intended as a scholarly study, it also includes some
flashes of narrative anarchy as a matter of policy. At different points it was
necessary to inject elements suggestive of action, color, and speed to avoid
encroaching boredom and serious depletion of the brain cell count. The idea
was to connect serious scholarship with a gonzo energy and style--at least in
places. However, it was neither possible nor desirable to keep it light, keep
it bright, and keep it moving in every section. The result is that the narrative
trends much more towards the sober and serious than to drama and color.

ACKNOWLEDGMENTS

A number of people provided the support, encouragement, and information
which made this book possible. Their contributions took many forms, but
always involved a willingness to sacrifice or share some of their time on my
behalf.
Robert Perrucci encouraged me to "just do it." I thought he meant to
take some chances in linking the study of occupational health policy to

professions, organizations, and politics. So I did, and I am grateful for his advice and encouragement.

I would especially like to thank the many informants who made this project possible. Although their voices are anonymous in this manuscript, I know and remember them individually. In almost every instance they were more generous with their time than I had any right to expect, and they provided me with a wealth of information that would have been otherwise unobtainable. I deeply appreciate the many courtesies they extended to me, especially during my visit to Washington, D.C.

My family also deserves special recognition and my gratitude for their endurance while the book was in progress. To Janet, Kristi, and Heather, I offer a special "thanx" for your singular patience, tireless support, and the many sacrifices which you have made on my behalf.

My colleague and friend David Wright provided excellent technical assistance during the preparation of the manuscript. Together we speed-lashed the project at a fast and terrible pace through more format changes than I care to count. However, David's style, tone, and computer savvy made it feel easy. Every author should be so fortunate to have such a keyboard wizard for a pal.

Finally, I would like to acknowledge the financial support of the Purdue Research Foundation and the National Science Foundation. These organizations provided important contributions which made the research possible.

High Risk and High Stakes

1

PROFESSIONAL SOCIETIES AND POLICY ISSUES

Professional . . . organizations . . . are part of whatever
societal transformations are underway. Solutions to problems
cannot be accomplished without their input.
                                          Bingham, et al., 1981, p. 13.

All professions . . . are . . . conspiracies against the laity.
                                   George Bernard Shaw, 1954, p. 17.

OCCUPATIONAL HEALTH POLICY:
IDEALS AND REALITIES

The juxtaposition of the promises of the Occupational Safety and Health Act
of 1970 (OSH Act) for workers' health with the persistence of deadly working
conditions for millions of Americans in the 1990s illustrates the continuing
tension between cultural ideals and political realities in this policy domain.
The OSH Act established as federal policy the right of workers to "a place of
employment free from recognized hazards that are causing or are likely to
cause death or serious physical harm."[1] To implement this right and oversee
its detailed administration, the OSH Act created the Occupational Safety and
Health Administration (OSHA) within the U.S. Department of Labor.[2]
Despite the ideals and structure embodied in the law, the reality shows the
level of harm inflicted by occupational health and safety hazards upon workers
continues to act as a profound influence upon societal-wide patterns of
morbidity and mortality. Conservative estimates place the annual death and
disability toll in the United States from occupational diseases at approximately
100,000 and 390,000 respectively (U.S. Congress: OTA Report 1985:37).

The reasons for this generation-long disparity between policy ideals and
workplace realities are widely recognized as political in nature. Numerous
authors have documented the struggle between industry and labor over the

implementation of the OSH Act and the mismatch of resources between the contending sides (Page and O'Brien 1973; Ashford 1976; Berman 1978; Kelman 1981; Navarro 1984; Szasz 1984; Noble 1986; Mendeloff 1988; Robinson and Paxman 1991). One consequence of this research has been to center attention upon those organizational actors most visibly and centrally involved in these struggles. This has resulted in an overwhelming research emphasis upon the interests, resources, and activities of consequential actors[3] such as corporations, labor unions, and peak associations[4] representing these groups (e.g., the U.S. Chamber of Commerce, the National Association of Manufacturers [NAM], the AFL-CIO), as well as various government agencies such as OSHA and the National Institute for Occupational Safety and Health (NIOSH).

PROFESSIONAL SOCIETIES:
A HISTORY OF NEGLECT

While the research on occupational health issues has clearly underscored the polarized, class-like character of the politics and power divisions in this policy arena, it has also largely ignored the policy-related interests and activities of health and safety professionals' associations. On the basis of the expressed purposes of these organizations and the scattered, limited research available, it is evident that they possess both demonstrated interests and concentrations of significant resources (i.e., expertise, money, personnel) relevant to developing occupational health and safety policies. Despite these attributes, little research concerning their policy involvement has appeared in the literature since the brief, summary accounts of their congressional testimony presented during the OSH Act hearings of 1968-1969 (Page and O'Brien 1973; Ashford 1976; Berman 1978).

The importance of medical and health science information and expertise to raising (and to a lesser extent resolving) occupational health and safety policy issues has been frequently noted. For example, Noble (1986:77) observes:

> The public health professionals and medical doctors who worked with unions and the rank-and-file workers were particularly influential [in the movement for occupational health and safety reform] . . . Dr. Selikoff's study made asbestos a national issue. Drs. Hawey Mills and Lorin Kerr did the same for black lung. Dr. E.I. Buff helped publicize the hazards of cotton dust.

Noble's focus, like that of most other investigators, illustrates that when the links between medical and health science information and policy development are considered, the emphasis has centered primarily upon the activities or contributions of either individual experts and/or ad hoc panels/advocacy groups of physicians and/or health scientists (e.g., Bazelon 1977, 1979; Sidel and Sidel 1984; Brickman et al. 1985; Badaracco 1985; Judkins 1986; Mendeloff 1988). Systematic inquiries into the involvement of health and safety professional associations on national policy issues are virtually nonexistent in the period from approximately the mid-1970s through the 1980s. In short, while the importance of the cultural authority[5] of health scientists' expertise to the occupational health and safety policy-making process is widely regarded as an important (though frequently contested) factor related to policy development and outcomes, the existing literature addressing the participation of associations of health and safety professionals in these matters is seriously deficient.

The extent of the neglect of professional associations by sociological investigators is underscored by Halliday's (1987:xiii) observation that "Professional associations are one of sociology's least-researched phenomena." More specifically, the deficiencies of research related to the links between these organizations and the development of national legislation are highlighted by Freidson (1986:191): "when one examines the literature on interest groups and lobbying in Washington, the professional associations are not very conspicuous. Only one--the American Medical Association--is mentioned with some frequency."

Although research interest in professional societies and other types of nonprofit organizations has increased in recent years (DiMaggio and Anheier 1990), sociological studies of the involvement of professional associations in the national policy-making process are still relatively rare. This book points the way towards redressing the long-standing neglect of research in this area. More specifically, it provides openings and clues for resolving some key issues addressed by Freidson (1986) concerning the unknowns related to association involvement with controversial policy issues. In a commentary on this subject Freidson (1986:196-97) notes (paradoxically) that "the very diversity of . . . [professional association] membership may . . . prevent them from . . . adopting any public position at all on controversial issues . . . [However,] this does not mean that professional associations cannot undertake any activities of significance." Freidson's observations raise an important question: What are the crucial factors that constrain or facilitate association action on significant and controversial public issues? While we really do not know at this point, this book moves us closer to empirically based answers to these kinds of questions.

PROFESSIONS, PROFESSIONALS, AND FOCAL ACTORS

In the sociological literature the definitions of profession and professional are variable (Freidson 1984) and are part of an extensive collection of both theoretical and empirical work concerning the sociology of professions (e.g., Parsons 1939; Freidson 1970a; Auerbach 1976; Berlant 1976; Larson 1977; Dingwall and Lewis 1983; Haskell 1984). A consideration of the numerous and complex issues which this literature addresses is beyond the scope of this inquiry. For our purposes, however, the health and safety professions are limited to and defined as the seven associations chosen as the focus of attention in this book. Although training, credentials, autonomy, prestige, and income vary widely among members of these associations, members all share the common bond of being full-time *specialists* concerned with the health and safety of workers and/or adult patients (who are virtually always either workers or former workers).

The seven associations referred to as the focal actors include (in the order of the size of their memberships according to the *1989 Encyclopedia of Associations*): (1) the American Medical Association (AMA), 271,000; (2) the American Public Health Association (APHA), 31,500; (3) the American Society of Safety Engineers (ASSE), 21,000; (4) the American Association of Occupational Health Nurses (AAOHN), 11,500; (5) the American Industrial Hygiene Association (AIHA), 7,500; (6) the American Occupational Medical Association (AOMA), 4,000; (7) the American Conference of Governmental Industrial Hygienists (ACGIH), 3,000 (Koek et al. 1988).

These groups were selected as the focus of attention for several reasons. First, the central, professional interests of these organizations (and their members) are directly related to occupational health and safety policy concerns; therefore, they possess the cultural authority of medical and/or scientific expertise in this area. Second, they all endorse and subscribe to formal codes of ethics which officially and publicly place the public interest and the health of workers above all other considerations or concerns; these claims raise questions about the extent to which ethical ideals influence the policy-related activities of these groups. Third, all of these organizations have past histories of involvement in various forums in the development of national occupational health and safety policies (Berman 1978; Noble 1986); thus, their previous organizational activities are indicative of their ongoing interests in public policy developments in this area.

HIGH RISK LEGISLATION

The High Risk Occupational Disease Notification and Prevention Act (High Risk Act/legislation) was selected as a vehicle for investigating the policy decisions of the seven associations for several reasons. First, outside of the mining industry, it has the distinction of being the only major national legislative reform effort in occupational health and safety policy since the OSH Act. In the 1968-88 period the OSH Act and the High Risk bills were the only two major legislative reform initiatives with provisions to broadly and generally strengthen federal protection for workers against occupational health and safety hazards to be seriously considered and/or passed by the Congress.[6]

Second, because the High Risk legislation is an example of controversial liberal reform,[7] it produced a highly polarized division of supporters and opponents. Organizations representative of labor were broadly arrayed in favor of the legislation, and those of business were solidly opposed (at least initially). As each side sought to legitimate its position with scientific and medical support, the professional associations were under pressure to add their cultural authority to the competing claims of each position; thus, this legislation provides a unique and rare opportunity for inquiring into the structural and contextual factors related to the focal actors' support for, opposition to, or neutrality towards occupational health and safety policy reforms.

Third, while professional associations' interest in and attempts to influence legislation favorable to their members' economic interests have received some research attention (e.g., Feldstein 1977, 1987; Freidson 1986; Keiser and Jones 1986; Tierney 1987), much less is known about the involvement of these organizations in controversial occupational health policy legislation. We know very little about the nature of the incentives or constraints that affect the decision-making processes within professional societies in such polarized policy struggles. The High Risk legislation provides an opportunity to explore this neglected aspect of professional associations' policy-related interests and activities.

RECURRING ISSUES AND THEMES

In the course of addressing the basic questions guiding the research, three major issues (and related concepts) serve as recurring themes which anchor and inform the narrative at various points throughout the book. They include the meaning of health policy and health politics, the interrelated topics of the influence of ethics and organizational interests upon the autonomy of professional societies, and the involvement of the health and/or medicine professions in social reform. Collectively, these issues not only assist in directing the inquiry, but they are also central to the general objectives of the study in the sense of developing a more complete understanding of the relationship between professionals, organizations, and social change.

Health Policy and Health Politics

Many studies on health policy have employed multiple operational definitions as well as numerous implicit (and often unexamined) assumptions regarding the meaning of this term. One of the major problems of much of this literature has been a tendency to equate health policy with government interventions centered around the organization, delivery, accessibility, and quality of health services (e.g., Stevens 1971; Mechanic 1972; Alford 1975; Thompson 1981; Kronenfeld and Whicker 1984; Laumann and Knoke 1987). Despite this tendency, there is also a developing body of literature emphasizing the need to expand the conceptualization of health policy. Several authors have pointed the way towards redefining health policy to include a consideration of concepts such as varying types of disease prevention (e.g., primary, secondary, tertiary),[8] and distinctions among the policy strategies (and political implications) of health promotion and health protection[9] (e.g., Milio 1981, 1988; Ratcliffe et al. 1984; Ratcliffe and Wallack 1985-86; Terris 1987; Levine and Lilienfeld 1987; Tesh 1988; Epstein 1990).

This shift towards a redefinition of health policy as a multidimensional concept generates important consequences in terms of requiring a more fine-grained approach to specific features of the different facets of health policy and the types of politics associated with each dimension of the health policy formation process. A useful point of departure for adding clarity to this developing trend is Lowi's (1964:689) suggestion that it is helpful to classify public policies in general terms on the basis "of their impact or expected impact on the society." Lowi's approach leads to the identification of three basic categories or types of public policy: distributive, regulatory, and redistributive. In the context of this discussion, distributive and redistributive categories are especially useful to analyses of health policy. They call attention to the effects that various types of policies may have upon the distribution or redistribution of scarce resources. This is an important distinction for as Lowi (1964:689-690) notes "each arena tends to develop its own characteristic political structure, political process, elites and group relations."

Analyses of health policy focusing primarily upon the organization or distribution of health services have developed insights and generalizations regarding the policy formation and legitimation processes centered around *distributive* policies and politics (e.g., Rohrer 1987). This means that health policies, when defined in the narrow sense of health services, have often been viewed as involving the distribution of government-financed benefits (usually directly to health service providers) without much controversy save for the amounts of the payments to health service providers. One consequence of such a focus has been to define health politics as typically involving organizational interests and configurations characterized as "cozy" or "iron triangles." In such arrangements the interests and goals of concerned interest groups, congressional subcommittees, and relevant government agencies are interpreted as intersecting in a symbiotic fashion. The organizational units are viewed as mutually rewarding to one another, and policy developments are managed by these elites without much public scrutiny or involvement (Gais, Peterson, and Walker 1984; Peters 1986).[10] A related consequence of this approach has been the consideration of occupational health and safety policy issues as falling within the domain of labor issues rather than within the health policy arena per se.

The Politics of Redistributive Policies

In contrast to the distributive research tradition, our approach views occupational health and safety issues as an integral dimension of health policy; however, it is a view which requires attention to a very different set of political dynamics. Policies aimed at the level of either primary or secondary disease prevention of work-related health problems via *health protection* strategies are considered as exemplifying *redistributive* public policies. As Lowi (1964:691) indicates, policies which fall within this category typically involve "the haves and the have-nots . . . proletariat and bourgeoisie." This condition occurs because the effects of redistributive policies produce the transfer of resources from those groups which possess resource concentrations to those groups which are resource deficient. The result of the politics of redistribution is not the creation of "cozy triangles" of mutual beneficiaries. Rather, the consequences involve reductions in resource inequalities among some segments of the society at the expense of other, resource-rich groups. Policies of this type embody the very essence of the idea of social policy (i.e., reductions of resource inequalities in society [Titmuss 1959; Korpi 1983]).

The basic idea of occupational health and safety policies reforms like the High Risk legislation involves shifting some of the health costs of work *away* from workers (in terms of work-induced illnesses and income losses). This shift forces corporate employers to absorb the costs of protecting worker health via modifications to the work setting and/or through employer-paid programs for monitoring, detecting, and treating work-induced illnesses.[11] To the extent that employers are forced to absorb even a fraction of the health-related costs of hazardous work environments, it is clear that an economic redistributive effect would be operative (Vogel 1983).

In addition to their economic redistributive features, occupational health policy reforms like the High Risk Act also tend to embody the potential for redistributive effects at the ideological[12] and political levels. Viewed as a form of symbolic politics (Edelman 1964, 1979, 1988), the High Risk Act (like the OSH Act before it) can be seen as emblematic of the ideological struggle between labor and business concerning the legitimacy of each side's interpretation of what constitutes the appropriate role of the state in advancing and/or protecting the interests of labor or business as well as what constitutes an equitable division of political power between the two groups. From this perspective, the High Risk Act, by mandating federal actions to protect workers' health, would provide evidence to workers that labors' ideological views and political interests (and the labor policy agenda) are legitimate (vis-a-vis corporate interests). If passed, such legislation would have the effect of adding state legitimacy to labor's views and interests and underscore the important lesson that in redistributive policy struggles, labor can succeed both ideologically and politically (Calavita 1983). From the perspective of employers, the ideological and political redistributive potential of the High Risk Act can be seen as posing significant threats to corporate interests. The High Risk legislation can be seen as a challenge to the legitimacy of business claims that current policy arrangements for protecting workers' health are adequate and that business interests in matters of occupational health are synonymous with the public interest. Furthermore, because the legislation would be likely to produce political empowering effects for workers, it would create the potential for a redistribution of the existing division of political power between business and labor.

Organizational struggles over the formation and implementation of redistributive policies with economic and ideological and/or symbolic politics dimensions are more likely to involve intense, class-like conflicts than is the case with distributive policies. Moreover, redistributive policies are also more likely to produce organizational outcomes characterized by deeply divided, polarized centers of competing interest groups and coalitions as "stakeholders" in the policy process (Shadish 1987:97) rather than "iron triangles" (Vogel 1980, 1983; Gais, Peterson, and Walker 1984). Indeed, as Marmor (1973:107) has pointed out, redistributive policies "reallocate benefits and burdens . . . [and] foster polarized and enduring conflict in which large national pressure groups play central roles."

Our insistence that occupational health policies be considered as an important dimension of health policy studies and of the need to explicitly focus upon the redistributive features of these policies opens the way to both an expanded and more precise understanding of the political dynamics of the health policy formation process. This approach allows us to understand that health policies that include primary and/or secondary prevention features and redistributive qualities are likely to produce different incentives and patterns of involvement in the policy formation process among health and safety professionals' associations than would be the case if the research focus was only upon distributive types of health policies where the provision of and payment for treatment-based health services were central issues. Identifying the incentives and constraints which impact upon the legislative participation activities among the focal actors in this case (as well as the structures and processes through which these factors operate) are among the major theoretical and research concerns of the book.

Ethics, Interests, Autonomy, and Policy

Fragmentary evidence from various sources indicates that professional societies can exercise significant influence in the policy-formation process. This means that their positions concerning health policy issues and the resources that they commit (or withhold) in support of their decisions represent important factors potentially capable of influencing the course of public debate and opinion (Miller 1972; Berman 1978; Noble 1986). The significance of professional societies to public policy development is emphasized by Bingham et al. (1981:13): "Professional . . . organizations . . . are part of whatever societal transformations are underway. Solutions to problems cannot be accomplished without their input." Waldo (1973:308) carries this theme even further: "Their personal, private, and often nongovernmental bases on one hand, and their public functions and orientation on the other make them key 'hinge' institutions."

The reality of the influence of professional societies upon the development of the High Risk legislation was frequently noted in several interviews in this study. For example, a senior lobbyist for the business coalition opposed to the High Risk bills commented:

> In this debate at least, the professional associations carried a lot of clout. I mean, depending on what side they came down on did make a difference. . . . Ah, they were not perceived as having a kind of hidden agenda which both labor and business is often accused of. [Some] of the key Senators also perceived them as quite important and I don't think I'm alone in that perception.

While we are not directly concerned with assessing the extent to which professional associations influence the policy-making process, the point here is to illustrate that they are important to this process. If we accept this view, then it is important to consider the issues of ethics, interests, and autonomy. That is, we need to examine how ethical considerations and the organizational interests of professional societies facilitate or constrain their potential to act with autonomy (vis-a-vis external interests) where public policy issues are concerned.

Ethics Versus Interests

The tension between the ethical claims of professional societies and the fact that they often appear to act in ways which protect their members' economic interests underscores the reality of goal conflicts among these organizations. For example, it is clear that, on one hand, professional associations are organized and motivated to act as monopoly agents. They attempt to structure the labor market for members' services as favorably as possible (often by cooperating with other organizations). As Freidson (1986:186) notes, "it attempts to protect and advance the fortunes of its members." On the other hand, the legitimacy of professional associations is grounded in claims of disinterested ethical commitments to clients and/or to public or community service. In fact, this service ideal is, according to Wilensky (1964:140), "the pivot around which the moral claim to professional status revolves."

The development of ethical codes and formal goals related to disinterested community service have been historically viewed by sociologists as central, distinguishing features of the professions (e.g., Carr-Saunders and Wilson 1933; Goode 1960; Durkheim 1964; Wilensky 1964). However, while the existence of such altruistic codes is real enough, their actual influence upon either the behavior of individual practitioners or the professional societies as organizations is both unknown and, at the same time, suspect.

As Freidson (1970b:81) has pointed out, little is known about the impact of altruistic ethical codes upon professional behavior. Empirical evidence for ardent identification with and strong support for ethical goals and service orientations among professionals does not currently exist (Larson 1977:59; Halliday 1987:xiv). Although little is known about the impact of ethical ideals upon the policies of professional societies, sociologists tend to treat them as facades for concealing economic self-interests. For example, Collins (1979:136-137) emphasizes the role of ethical codes in legitimizing professional self-interest: "Codes of ethics . . . serve quite well to reinforce a restrictive club . . . to prevent competition, and thereby to keep fees high."

Suspicions regarding the motives and interests of professionals and professional associations are threaded through much of the recent sociological work on the professions. While these critiques vary widely in tone and emphases, a common theme running through much of this literature is that formal ethical codes and community service statements are not to be taken seriously as guidelines for understanding the goals and activities of professionals or their organizations where policy issues are concerned. Economic self-interest is more frequently viewed as the true goal of the professions, with many authors apparently willing to concur that "professions differ from trade unions only in their sanctimoniousness" (Freidson 1970b:367)

Interests and Autonomy

Since it appears that the involvement of professional societies in policy issues is widely suspected as being influenced less by ethics and more by economic self-interests, it is then important to ask: To what extent are associations' self-interests conditioned by linkages to external constituencies? While it may not be surprising to find that professional societies tend to pursue policy agendas which serve their members' interests, we also need to ask: To what extent are they pursuing these interests independently? That is, are these organizations autonomous agents or, where policy issues are concerned, do they act in conjunction with and perhaps on behalf of the interests of other, external actors or constituencies? In order to answer these questions it is necessary to clarify how the interests of professional associations may be structurally intertwined with the interests of other organizations and/or constituencies and explore how such linkages may impact upon their ethical commitments and autonomy. These questions highlight how the involvement of professional societies in the health policy reform process could take very different directions depending upon the extent to which the organizations are autonomous or linked to the interests of other groups.

Autonomy and Policy

If we accept the view that professional societies are at least potentially influential actors in the policy-formation process, then the direction of their involvement with specific legislative reforms becomes a matter of real importance. For example, the active engagement of these associations on behalf of policy reforms such as the High Risk legislation could potentially facilitate a swifter introduction of life-saving and health-protective programs and policies. At the same time, active opposition to such policies could potentially contribute to the continuation of current, unsafe and/or dangerous working conditions. Speaking to the linkages between public health hazards, public policies, and the role of professional associations, Miller (1972:248) observes: "One can speculate that earlier statements by respected societies of knowledgeable specialists could have forestalled the advance of dangerous developments, reduced the magnitude of damage, and forced the swifter initiation of remedial measures."

Despite the positive health benefits that could result from the active involvement of professional societies on behalf of public and/or occupational health policy reform legislation, these organizations have seldom taken the lead for such causes (Miller 1972; Page and O'Brien 1973; Brodeur 1974; Ashford 1976; Berman 1978; Noble 1986). More often than not, a position of silence or neutrality has characterized the approach of many professional associations to controversial health policy reforms (especially in the early stages of such legislation).

On the face of it, policies of neutrality might appear to be indicative of organizational autonomy. However, when professional organizations remain neutral on policy issues, these nondecisions can be interpreted as representing a kind of covert support for the status quo (or existing policies). As Miller (1972:247) points out:

> When a scientific society [elects] to remain aloof from taking a stand on a . . . question, it has, in fact taken an influential stand on that question. . . . Whatever a scientific society may think it is doing or not doing in relation to public policy in the current state of affairs, the end result is a *de facto* position, and likely to be one of considerable importance. . . . The message transmitted by silence on an issue of debatable public policy is clear. It has the force of a tacit endorsement.

Miller's observation makes it clear that so-called neutral association policy positions are not likely to be neutral in terms of their policy effects. In fact, as we will see, such positions are more likely to be indicators not of organization neutrality and autonomy, but rather of a kind of covert policy of opposition and a relative *lack* of organizational autonomy.

Bachrach and Baratz (1970) have also pointed out how organizational policy positions of neutrality may be understood as supportive of the status quo and reflective of what they call "a mobilization of bias." This concept refers to the idea that organizational nondecisions are often illustrative of subtle conformity by less powerful groups to a set of institutional controls established by other, more powerful entities which have an interest in maintaining the status quo. Bachrach and Baratz (1970:7) point out that "Power is . . . exercised when *A* devotes his energies to creating or reinforcing social and political values and institutional practices that limit the scope of the political process to public consideration of only those issues which are comparatively innocuous to *A*."

Insofar as professional associations and policy-involvement activities are concerned, the preceding considerations remind us that we cannot assume autonomy or take impartiality for granted. Rather, we must be alert to the possibility that association policy positions may reflect deeply entrenched and perhaps socially accepted or even taken-for-granted (or possibly hidden) material and/or ideological connections with other, more powerful external organizational entities or constituencies.

Health Professionals and Reform

Health and medicine have frequently served as focal points of reference for numerous sociological inquires concerned with the nature, role, and power of the professions in American society (e.g., Freidson 1970a, 1970b, 1985, 1986, 1989; Brown 1979; Derber 1982, 1983; Starr 1982; McKinlay 1982; McKinlay and Arches 1985). However, much of this research has been focused upon relatively abstract concerns. These include issues such as the meaning of professions, the processes of professionalization, deprofessionalization, and proletarianization, and finally, the "new class debates"[13] concerning the extent to which individual professionals are likely to act as agents for reform.

Much of this research has painted a rather gloomy picture of the commitment of the health professions on behalf of progressive social reforms. For example, health professionals have often been viewed as opposing progressive social reforms as a result of narrow self-interests and/or allegiances to elite groups in the society (Freidson 1970b, Illich 1976; Brown 1979; Navarro 1986). At the same time, another strand of this research has suggested that health professionals are increasingly being stripped of autonomy and power by market forces transforming medicine from a cottage industry into institutional capitalism (Starr 1982; McKinlay and Arches 1985; Feinglass and Salmon 1990). Implicit in this scenario is the inference that health professionals *may*, at some point, react politically to the erosion of professional autonomy and power by identifying with the interests of workers and become more supportive of progressive social policy legislation. However, this view is speculative as a long-term possibility and does not suggest that a departure from the conservative political traditions is anything close to an immediate prospect.

In this study the linkage between health and medicine, professionals, and reform is also a focal point of concern, but the research emphasis is shifted away from abstract and/or individualized issues to very specific and tangible topics and organizations. Targeting the policy-involvement activities of a particular group of professional societies regarding specific reform legislation allows us to refine our understanding of the interests and power of health professionals as agents of reform in contemporary society--at least insofar as their organizations are concerned.

As noted earlier, the issue of the extent to which the interests of health professionals are likely to lead to support for progressive legislative reforms has seldom been framed and addressed via examinations of the policy-oriented activities of their *organizations*. Our exploration of the involvement of these organizations within the context of developments in a conflicted, redistributive policy arena provides a new angle for developing insights into professionals' interests and unity on social policy issues. This approach advances our understanding of whether (or under what conditions) professional groups act as a force promoting social reforms; it also enhances our awareness of the extent to which (and reasons why) professionals are a unified or divided force for social change today. This latter point is of interest to Marxist analysts because it is concerned with the extent to which professionals occupy "contradictory-class locations,"[14] which lead to inconsistent behavioral outcomes in terms of policy support or opposition (Oppenheimer 1985). More specifically, the focus upon professional organizations allows for an enhanced understanding of the extent to which (and under what conditions) professional groups may be expected to act independently or as coalitional partners with either business or labor organizations in supporting or opposing occupational health policy reform legislation.

OVERVIEW

This chapter has identified the professional associations and the occupational health policy legislation, which are the core concerns of the book. It has also outlined recurring issues related to occupational health legislation as a redistributive policy issue, the importance of examining the policy involvement of the focal actors with the High Risk legislation in terms of possible interest linkages with external constituencies, and the extent to which and conditions under which organizations of health professionals may act as agents for reform.

Chapter 2 both outlines the theoretical and methodological orientations that guide the research and presents two research hypotheses regarding the influence of interorganizational linkages upon the focal actors' involvement with the High Risk legislation.

Chapter 3 traces the historical development of risk notification as a concept and developing policy from the pre-OSHA period to 1985. In chapter 4 we track the progress of the High Risk bills over the 1985-88 period and examine the details of the political struggles associated with the bills. Chapter 5 begins with an overview of key structural characteristics of the seven associations and also includes data summaries relevant to assessing the research hypotheses developed in chapter 2.

Chapters 6 and 7 consist of positive and negative case narratives. Chapter 6 describes the activities of the four associations that supported the High Risk legislation. Chapter 7 details the actions of the three associations that were neutral towards or opposed to it. Both chapters also include accounts of the role played by contextual factors in shaping the details of the associations' policy decisions on the legislation.

Chapter 8 summarizes the results of the research, revisits key issues outlined in chapter 1, and offers some general conclusions based upon the research. This final chapter also includes suggestions for future research agendas related to understanding the interests of professional societies, interorganizational linkages, and legislative reform.

2

ORGANIZATIONS, THEORY, AND HEALTH POLICY

> Follow the money . . . Just follow the money.
>
> Advice of anonymous source, "Deep Throat," to reporter Bob Woodward in the Watergate case, *All The President's Men*, 1974.[1]

INTRODUCTION

In 1991 the American Association of Retired Persons (AARP) was described as "[the] well-paid lackey of the health insurance industry" by the Public Citizen Health Research Group (HRG) (*Health Letter* 1991:12). The HRG (one of Ralph Nader's organizations) indictment of AARP was based on its failure to endorse a growing health care reform movement in the United States favoring a Canadian-style, single-payer National Health Program. The clear implication was that the failure of AARP to do so was related to its steep green connection to the insurance industry. During 1986-89, AARP received $348 million from the Prudential Insurance Company of America for assisting in marketing Prudential's group health insurance to AARP members. The money amounted to "more than one-third--34.8 percent--of AARP operating revenues during those years" (*Health Letter* 1991:12). Despite the AARP image as a defender of the interests of older Americans, the HRG report clearly called the organization's priorities and commitments into question. It concluded by noting that it is "not [surprising that] the leadership of AARP is more responsive to its big business ties to Prudential than to the need of its thirty million members for a much better health care system" (*Health Letter* 1991:12).

Implicit in the *Health Letter* report is a theory of organizational behavior whereby important resource linkages influence organizational policy decisions. In many respects the theory guiding the present study derives from the basic idea behind the HRG's interpretation of AARP's policy on health care reform.

While our theoretical approach is more elaborately detailed and explicitly stated, the central thesis remains similar to the underlying political-economy approach taken in the HRG critique.

As noted in chapter 1, research into the involvement of professional societies on national policy issues represents a relatively unexplored area. The limited state of both theory and research related to the organizational behavior of professional associations provides little guidance on how to proceed. Consequently, both the theoretical and methodological approaches adopted in this study include orienting and developmental dimensions. That is, the inquiry is directed by a coherent core of orienting concepts derived from organizational theory to provide guidance in a causal/analytic sense; yet at the same time, the inquiry remains open to the potential for evidence-derived discoveries which might lead to grounded theoretical insights and constructs (Glaser and Strauss 1967). The methodology consists of a dual-level approach. The central feature is a variation of a case-oriented comparative design (Ragin 1987) used to assess the extent to which interorganizational linkages influenced the policy involvement decisions of the seven associations regarding the High Risk legislation; also, in order to address the role of contextual factors in the policy-making process, a second, more general, case-study style approach is used (Yin 1984).

ORGANIZATIONAL BEHAVIOR AND STRUCTURE

For purposes of clarity, it is useful to preface the specific features of our organizational behavior model with an outline of key assumptions and orienting ideas which undergird our general theoretical approach. We begin with the observation that while organization behavior can be understood in terms of multiple perspectives (e.g., Pfeffer 1982:1-40), our general approach is essentially structural. We assert that the organizational behavior of professional societies can best be understood as a consequence of structural factors that condition their interests and which also intersect with and influence the decisions of those individuals who function as organizational decision makers on matters of policy. By structural factors we refer to the idea that like the AARP, these organizations are embedded within both wider and more potent organizational and political-economy environments. This wider context shapes and influences interests of professional associations as well as their potential for survival and growth. While professional societies did not create this context, they cannot ignore it or their positions in it. Their leaders and members must take the structural context and their location in it into account and adapt to the economic, political, and cultural realities it presents; this is especially true where controversial, redistributive public policy issues are concerned.

The Health Policy-Making Process: Orienting Propositions

Our assumptions and views concerning the nature of the health policy formation process, the dynamics which drive it, and the cast of actors involved are summarized in the following six interrelated series of propositions. To begin, the occupational health policy-making process is assumed to be a largely organizational enterprise. Individuals are viewed as important primarily in relation to their being situated within positions that enable them to command, mobilize, or influence organizational resources which may be used to initiate, support, modify, or oppose legislative policy proposals. As Laumann and Knoke (1987:1, 4) observe, "State policies are the product of complex interactions among . . . organizations . . . . We see organizations rather than natural persons as the core actors at the [national] level of [policy making]."

Second, controversial, redistributive health policy issues (such as the High Risk bills) are viewed as involving a wide range of organizational participants distributed along a continuum of interest in, power to influence, and involvement with the legislation. Those organizations whose interests, power, and involvement place them at the center of such legislative struggles are conceptualized as *core actors* (e.g., corporations, organized labor, and their peak associations); other interested organizations are viewed as shading, by various degrees, into what we term *peripheral actors* (or peripheral actor groups--including professional associations). The core actors are viewed as involved in efforts to expand their influence on policy issues of great importance to their interests by developing formal and informal network ties to groups with similar interests. These networks are composed primarily of organizational allies but may also be considered as embracing individuals based in positions where they have access to or control over organizational resources and power. This core versus periphery imagery is adapted from various topics and sources including world systems theory (Wallerstein 1979), labor markets (Hodson and Kaufman 1982), and organizations and policy making (Laumann and Knoke 1987).

Third, governmental entities such as federal agencies and congressional committees are viewed as important arenas where the competing core actors struggle to create wider networks of influence. These organizations have various resources including the potential for conferring state legitimacy upon the policy preferences of the core actors. Decisions regarding how these resources are to be deployed are viewed as depending upon complex political relationships that exist between governmental entities and core actor organizations in terms of financial and legal linkages as well as personnel ties involving ideological affinities and allegiances. This image of government as an arena where business-labor conflicts are conducted with varying degrees of support from governmental entities for each side is consistent with conceptualizations of the state as developed by various authors (e.g., Mills 1956; Domhoff 1978, 1983, 1987; Useem 1978, 1984; Navarro 1991).

Fourth, the political struggles related to issues such as the High Risk legislation involve a dynamic process whereby competing core actor groups or networks seek to maximize their chances for resolving issues on terms most favorable to their interests. This includes, among other actions, attempting to exercise their influence upon governmental entities such as congressional committees and by efforts to recruit potentially interested or expert organizations as political allies from among the peripheral actors. This view is similar to and intersects with some of the general ideas of resource mobilization theory (e.g., Gamson 1975; McCarthy and Zald 1977; Jenkins 1983).

Fifth, the success of competing core actors in attracting peripheral actors to support their policy positions is viewed as tied in important ways to the linkages that peripheral actors have with resource bases and constituencies which predispose their interests in and sympathies for the positions of the core actors. Specifically, the greater the number and extent of linkages between core and peripheral actors, the more closely the positions of the two groups are likely to converge on controversial policy issues. This general proposition is derived from interorganizational and network-style analyses (e.g., Benson 1975; Zeitz 1980; Knoke and Kuklinski 1982; Galaskiewicz 1985; Marsden 1990).

Finally, contextual events and/or circumstances (only some of which fall within the reach of core actors' influence) in both the internal and external organizational environments (of both core and peripheral actors) are also viewed as important to the policy process. These factors constitute a kind of wild card capable of influencing organizational alignments in important, but less predictable, ways among core and peripheral actors and, hence, policy outcomes. The influence of contextual factors upon organizational behavior is considered to represent an important analytic dimension by several organizational analysts (e.g., Aldrich 1979; Perrow 1986; Laumann and Knoke 1987).

Considered collectively, these propositions create a view of the occupational health policy process as occurring within what Perrow (1986:192) characterizes as "a nested-box . . . environment." That is, the general political-economy forms the overall context within which the core actors are embedded and which generally conditions their actions. At the next level, the core actors create and sustain competing organizational networks that are distinct from, and far less general than, the overall political-economy. In the policy-making process, the activities of the core actor networks are viewed as focused upon efforts to influence and/or dominate relevant governmental units and entities, attract organizations from the periphery into their respective interest orbits on particular policy issues, and maintain internal cohesion within their own respective core networks.

The professional associations (as part of the peripheral actor group) are embedded first of all within the general political-economy. They are also subject to involvement in the dynamic organizational networks of the competing core actors which attempt to recruit them into legislative struggles on their respective sides. As was the case with the AARP example, a primary feature of this perspective is the view that the important factors structuring the policy-involvement decisions of professional associations are centered around interorganizational linkages which predispose their policy involvement on behalf of the interests and positions of the competing core actors. At the same time, contextual events and circumstances are also considered as having the potential to modify or reinforce the predisposing effects of the linkage ties.

The relevance and utility of an interorganizational or network perspective utilizing multiple levels of analysis in the study of organizational behavior is underscored by Perrow (1986:263-264):

> Our perspective indicates that we should always examine the possibility that organizational masters prefer unofficial goals over official ones and may even make sure that official goals are not achieved. We should then search for extra-organizational interests that are served by what appears to be, from a leadership perspective, drift or goal displacement. . . . By examining the organizational setting in which the organization functions, including the values available in the sector, we may find explanations for an apparent lack. . . of "proper" organizational practices.

ORGANIZATIONAL BEHAVIOR:
A POLITICAL MODEL AND HYPOTHESES

The preceding section should make it clear that our theoretical perspective emphasizes the view that organizational behavior is better understood "by using political models than rational decision-making models" (Perrucci et al. 1980:150). This approach suggests that organizations are somewhat analogous to "private governments" (Gilb 1966:109; Perrucci et al. 1980:150); consequently, organizational choices and policy decisions are viewed as occurring via essentially political processes which are reflective of dynamic linkages between internal policy-making groups and the interests and power[2] of various external constituencies and resource environments (Benson 1975; Zeitz 1980; Pfeffer 1982; Perrow 1986).

This view implies that organizational goals and policy choices are best understood as political outcomes. They reflect the power of a prevailing internal coalition to structure organizational policy in a fashion consistent with its perceptions of the *organization's* values and interests--especially as those interests are perceived as linked with those of external groups. The dominant internal coalition may be characterized as the "master or masters of the organization"[3] (Perrow 1986:261). The *masters* thus possess the necessary power and authority to formally and officially shape organizational policy and commit resources in support of policies which they favor.

A central feature of our model asserts that linkages tying professional societies to either the corporate sector or the nonprofit sector act as important channels of influence. These ties are viewed as especially significant in shaping the interests and policy decisions of the focal actors regarding the High Risk bills. This is held to be the case because legislation of this type essentially aims at enlarging the role of the state. Thus, it serves the interests of associations comprised mainly of state-employed professionals by enhancing their numbers and influence. At the same time, this type of legislation is likely to negatively impact the interests of corporations by increasing costs and constricting their autonomy; thus, professional associations with strong ties to this sector would be expected to reflect corporate views as a means of protecting the interests of their members who work in private sector firms.

The connections between the focal actors and the corporate and nonprofit sectors posited as having important effects upon association policy involvement decisions concerning the High Risk legislation are conceptualized in terms of three structural linkage factors: sponsorship, interpenetration, and resource dependency. In general, it is hypothesized that both the direction of the associations' basic policy positions regarding the High Risk legislation (i.e., support or opposition/neutrality) and the extent of organizational resources committed on behalf of their basic policy positions will be dependent upon the degree to which the associations, their members, and their leaders possess a relative freedom from direct dependence upon corporate enterprises for employment and organizational resources.

Following this general hypothesis, two more specific research hypotheses are explored. First, it is expected that association autonomy will be maximized by strong, multiple linkages to the nonprofit sector and that associations exhibiting such patterns will support the High Risk legislation; conversely, it is also expected that strong, multiple linkages to the corporate sector will minimize autonomy and associations exhibiting such linkage patterns will oppose (or be neutral towards) the legislation. Second, it is expected that the greater the consistency of strong, multiple linkages tying the focal actors with either the nonprofit or corporate sectors, the greater will be the extent of association support for or opposition to the High Risk legislation.

STRUCTURAL LINKAGE FACTORS

In the following three sections, subtypes of the three structural linkage factors are identified and discussed along with the rationale for their utilization. Subtype variations are denoted with pluses (+) and minuses (-) to identify those expected to be linked with association policies of support or neutrality/opposition (respectively) towards the High Risk legislation.

Sponsorship

Sponsorship (Derber 1983) identifies the economic sector where a *majority* of each association's membership is employed. Two sponsorship subtypes are identified: (1) Corporate (-), a majority of association members employed in for-profit corporations and/or acting as self-employed, small business operators. (2) Nonprofit (+), membership majorities employed in the public sector in locations such as universities, governmental agencies, and other nonprofit organizations.[4]

It is expected that the focal actors' policy and resource-commitment decisions regarding the High Risk legislation will be strongly influenced by the occurrence of specific sponsorship subtypes. The assumptions and logic supporting and justifying the use of this concept in developing a predictive scheme require some comment and clarification. First, it is assumed that because association policy makers (as "masters" of the organizations) are drawn from the membership, they are likely to be attitudinally both similar and responsive to the general, prevailing political views and values of the members in their organizations. Therefore, it is expected that the predominant political views and attitudes of the members will be reflected in association leadership policy and resource-commitment decisions. Also, insofar as the High Risk legislation is generally representative of liberal reform, we expect that those professional associations whose memberships' attitudes trend in a politically liberal direction would be more likely to be supportive of the legislation (and that the reverse condition would also obtain).

Previous research aimed at understanding the bases of political liberalism among professionals indicates that a general relationship exists between their political views and their employment sector locations (reconceptualized here as sponsorship) (Brint 1984, 1987). In general, the attitudinal research indicates that "political liberalism . . . varies *inversely* with the dependence of an individual's job on profit maximization" (emphasis in the original, Lamont 1987:1503). In short, professional employment in the nonprofit sector tends to be associated with liberal political views while professional employment in the private sector tends to be associated with more conservative political views.

This general relationship finds additional support in other studies concerning not only the political views and attitudes of individual health professionals (e.g., Lynn 1986), but also professional association policies as well (e.g., Peterson and Walker 1986). Commenting on their research, the latter two authors observe:

> Professional societies emerging from communities in the profit-making sector of the economy are more likely to call for a reduction in the size and influence of the federal government. Groups advocating a larger regulatory role for government and an expansion of social programs . . . emerge from occupational communities within the society's growing nonprofit realm. . . [In short,] the ideological positions of interest groups are closely related to the elements of the society they represent (Peterson and Walker 1986:171).

Although the volume of supportive research related to this topic is relatively thin, the studies that we do find are mutually reinforcing. The literature underscores the importance of the linkage between employment sponsorship and not only the political attitudes of individual professionals (including those in the health and medicine fields), but also the policy positions of their associations regarding liberal reforms. Thus, we expect that corporate sponsorship patterns will predispose professional association policy makers to favor the policies and interests of those core actors representing the business community. By contrast, we also expect the opposite situation to obtain. That is, nonprofit sponsorship patterns are expected to enhance association autonomy (vis-a-vis corporate interests and influence), predispose association policy-setting boards to endorse liberal policies, and produce alliances with core actors representing organized labor.

Interpenetration

Interpenetration (Halliday 1987) refers to personnel linkages whereby association officers and/or directors occupy paid, full-time positions in for-profit corporations at executive and/or administrative levels or types (i.e., positions involving relatively high levels of supervisory responsibilities, pay, and prestige). Two interpenetration subtypes are identified: (1) High Levels (-), percentages greater than 50 percent. (2) Low Levels (+), percentages less than 50 percent (or absent).[5]

The basic idea of interpenetration, as Halliday (1987:335) notes, "draws upon the Boolean algebra concept of intersecting sets, where members simultaneously participate in two or more overlapping organizations." Interpenetration is similar to the concept of interlocking directorates in organizational research related to capitalistic firms both in terms of form as well as the subtle processes through which organizational influence is exerted (e.g., Useem 1984; Palmer et al. 1986; Mizruchi 1987; Perrucci and Lewis 1989).

Since interpenetration is limited to the linkages tying (or not tying) association officers and/or directors to the corporate sector, those association leaders tied to corporations are viewed as embedded within a unique personnel network. Such a network is posited as bringing association "masters" into close contact with a wider set of co-workers and organizational entities which have strong and direct interests in the policy and resource-commitment decisions of the professional societies. This means that the policy decisions of typically unpaid and part-time association leaders are likely to be susceptible to formal and/or informal pressures to sculpt association policies on controversial legislation in such a fashion so as to cause them to conform to the general contours that match the interests of their corporate employers.

Because association leaders tend to possess elite characteristics (in terms of personal resources and prestige vis-a-vis average association members--e.g., Garceau 1941; Truman 1962; Gilb 1966; Halliday 1987), it is expected that officers and directors (especially where corporate sponsorship prevails) will be particularly likely to occupy positions at high levels of prestige and power in external, for-profit firms. Thus, as boundary-spanning groups, association leaders with elite characteristics are especially likely to embrace patterns of material interests and ideological affinities consonant with the elite leaders of the corporate firms where they are employed. This condition is expected to increase the likelihood that association policy decisions will trend in directions that favor (and further) the interests of external, employer organizations.

Although the interpenetration subtype links are directly observable, unfortunately, the processes through which influence is exerted are likely to be subtle and largely invisible in the sense of being open to direct observation and measurement (Palmer et al. 1986). However, it is assumed that these processes do exist and exert influence upon the policy choices of association officials. Specifically, we expect that high levels of interpenetration will be linked with association policies which tend to mirror and support those of the core actors representing the business community on the High Risk legislation. By contrast, we also expect that low levels of interpenetration (like nonprofit sponsorship) will enhance association autonomy and lead to support for the High Risk bills and coalitions with core actors representing organized labor.

26   High Risk and High Stakes

Resource Dependency

Resource Dependency (Pfeffer and Salancik 1978) is defined in terms of the
extent to which an association's annual revenue is derived from individual
membership dues versus other income sources. Three resource dependency
subtypes are identified: (1) External-Corporate (-), a majority of association
income derived from nondues sources combined with a corporate sponsorship
pattern; (2) External-Nonprofit(+), a majority of association income derived
from nondues sources combined with a nonprofit sponsorship pattern; (3)
Internal-Dependent (+), a majority of association income derived from
membership dues.[6]

Resource dependency, as a general theoretical orientation, suggests that
organizations (i.e., organizational "masters" as policy makers) must be
concerned with an adequate flow of resources, including money and authority
(Benson 1975). Moreover, dependent, resource-recipient organizations are
likely to structure their behaviors and policies in ways that are congruent with
the interests of their resource benefactors. As Pfeffer (1982:193) notes,
"organizational behavior becomes externally influenced because the focal
organization must attend to the demands of those in its environment that
provide resources necessary and important for its continued survival."

Even though professional associations are created and sustained by the
members and leaders for multiple reasons (including the potentially conflicting
goals of "monopoly"and "service"), clearly, their policy-making masters will and
must be concerned with the issue of resource procurement. Sufficient
resources are necessary in order for the leadership to address two core
organizational concerns: (1) survival (as a precondition for meeting any other
objectives--Gouldner 1959) and (2) effectiveness (i.e., in terms of meeting
membership needs and requirements--otherwise the members would cease to
support the organization and it would not survive--Gilb 1966). These realities
insure that the organizational masters will be extremely attentive to the
interests and views of those organizations whose resources are crucial to
funding the association's budget (as well as to sustaining and/or expanding the
association's [and the profession's] legitimacy and authority).

The general expectation concerning the effect of this factor is that
dependency subtypes will act as strong influences upon association policy
decisions. Associations exhibiting external-corporate dependency patterns are
expected to adopt policy positions consistent with those favored by core actors
representing the business community; by contrast, it is expected that
associations with external-nonprofit and internal-dependent patterns will be
more autonomous (vis-a-vis corporate interests) and inclined towards policy
decisions favorable to reform and hence to the interests and policies of core
actors representing organized labor.

ASSOCIATION POLICY AND
RESOURCE-COMMITMENT DECISIONS

Association policies concerning the High Risk legislation are conceptualized in terms of two dimensions: (1) Basic Policy Decisions and (2) Resource-Commitment Decisions. The former dimension consists of two possible policy positions: Support or Neutral/Opposed. The latter dimension, which is conceptualized as the *extent* of resources committed on behalf of the basic policy decisions, is divided into a continuum of decision levels or types ranging from strong support to neutrality and to strong opposition.

Basic Policy Decisions

The application of summary or global characterizations to organizations' basic policy positions on occupational health reform legislation derives from research related to the OSH Act. This research suggests that while the details of policy participation among organizational actors may change over time, their basic policy positions remain relatively stable (e.g., Page and O'Brien 1973; Berman 1978; Noble 1986).

The rationale supporting the grouping of basic policies of neutrality and opposition into a single category was noted earlier. In chapter 1 the works of Miller (1972) and Bachrach and Baratz (1970) were cited as illustrating how policy positions of neutrality among professional associations can legitimately be interpreted as positions supporting the status quo. In other words, not adopting a policy position (the silence of neutrality) represents a kind of *de facto* opposition to reform efforts. A neutral organizational position implies that no changes are viewed as necessary and serves as an implicit statement of opposition to change. Thus, we believe it is legitimate to combine neutral/opposed policy decisions into a single category.

For each association, basic policy decision subtypes towards the High Risk legislation were determined, to the extent possible, on the basis of publicly reported policy statements. Examples of policy statement sources include testimony provided by association representatives at congressional subcommittee hearings, published statements in association documents, interview data, and archival documents (such as correspondence). The criteria for collating different types of evidence in order to arrive at basic policy position subtypes sometimes involved qualitative interpretations, especially in those cases where the information appeared to be inconsistent or incomplete. However, this was not often the case. For the most part determinations of basic policy positions were based upon mutually reinforcing patterns of evidence from multiple sources which usually formed consistent and stable patterns.

Resource-Commitment Decisions

The extent of association resources committed on behalf of a basic policy position was divided into a continuum of typologies ranging from varying levels of support (strong, moderate, nominal), to neutrality, to varying levels of opposition (strong, moderate, nominal). The following diagram illustrates this approach:[7]

(1)			(2)		(3)	
Support			Neutrality		Opposition	
Strong	Moderate	Nominal		Nominal	Moderate	Strong
+ + +	+ +	+	=	-	- -	- - -

The small number of cases and wide variations in association characteristics and resources did not permit the use of a standardized, quantitative formula for computing values for the continuum typologies. Instead, qualitative assessments were utilized. The indicators informing the typologies included several factors.

1. The timing of association involvement with the legislation (i.e., were positions of support or opposition [or neutrality] expressed early [1985-86] or later [1987-88] in the development of the High Risk bills?)
2. The extent and continuity of personal contacts between association leadership/senior staff and congressional subcommittee members and staff concerning association policy positions towards the legislation (public or informal).
3. The participation (or lack thereof) of association representatives in the public hearings on the legislation.
4. The extent to which the focal actors allocated space in organizational publications (newsletters and journals) devoted to reporting on the High Risk legislation and in publicizing their policy positions towards the bills.
5. The extent to which the associations' leadership and/or senior staff were involved in efforts to mobilize the membership to support or oppose the legislation in a grassroots fashion (e.g., the encouragement of letter-writing campaigns to members of Congress).

6. Evidence of any financial support via association-sponsored political action committees (PACs) for members of Congress based upon their support for or opposition to the legislation.

Decisions concerning the collation of these factors and the assignment of resource-commitment level decisions to the seven associations were based upon an evolving and ongoing "dialogue with the evidence" (Ragin 1987:165). That is, as the evidence was collected and examined, mutually reinforcing patterns were identified, noted, and cross checked. Assessments of the involvement of the associations by personnel from core actor organizations and congressional subcommittee staff members regarding how helpful the associations were perceived to be in supporting or opposing the legislation throughout the period were especially helpful in developing informed judgments for each case. Through the application of these procedures, intersecting and corroborative evidence provided the primary basis for the qualitative assignment of the resource-commitment categories.

The application of the continuum typologies led to a stratified ordering of the seven associations that ranged from the most strongly supportive organization to the one that was most strongly opposed. This comparative listing, along with descriptive accounts of variations in resource-commitment levels, provides a useful means for assessing the relative influence of both structural linkages and contextual factors upon resource commitment decisions. Its application is consistent with similar kinds of research aimed at assessing decision outcomes of organizations through the use of multiple qualitative and quantitative indicators (e.g., Whitt 1979, 1982).

METHODS AND DATA

The Comparative Method

The qualitative, case-oriented comparative methodological dimension of the study (Skocpol 1984; Ragin 1987; McMichael 1990) views the focal actors as seven distinct cases. Such small numbers do not permit assessments of the posited effects of the structural linkage factors via conventional statistical techniques. Instead, the research hypotheses are explored via procedures utilizing variations of what Skocpol (1984) and Ragin (1987) have described as the "method of agreement" and "indirect method of difference."

The method of agreement involves examining cases which share common, similar outcomes (i.e., similar dependent variable results and/or values) to determine the extent to which they also share common patterns of posited causal factors. By contrast, the indirect method of difference involves comparing cases with divergent outcomes (i.e., dissimilar or opposite dependent variable results and/or values) as a means of determining the extent to which contrasting cases are also dissimilar in terms of posited causal factor patterns. These procedures allow us to examine the extent to which the predictions of the research hypotheses concerning the influence of structural linkages are supported by the data--even with a small sample population of seven cases.

The Contextual Dimension

An assessment of how and why contextual events or circumstances were important to the focal actors' involvement with the High Risk legislation (either separately or in conjunction with the structural linkage factors) was conducted via case-study style methods. These techniques were applied to develop an intimate acquaintance with the details of and the politics related to the High Risk legislation, and to identify and describe those contextual events and circumstances related (either directly or indirectly) to the interests and internal policy-making processes of the focal actors.

Although a full-scale case study of all dimensions of the High Risk legislation as a political issue and historical episode was beyond the scope of this inquiry, systematic efforts were made to identify and examine the central issues and major political events related to the case. These efforts were aimed at the development of a descriptive overview of the background, details, and political dynamics associated with the High Risk legislation.

In assessing the influence of contextual factors upon the seven associations' policy decisions, circumstances and events within the organizations' internal and external environments were considered. At the internal level, association politics were of special interest. An example of internal politically relevant events which might impact upon association policies on the High Risk bills would be the occurrence of any incidents of internal dissent regarding organizational policies on the legislation.

At the level of the external environment the focus was upon events and/or circumstances viewed as relevant to the associations' internal policy-making processes. Contextual factors of special interest in the external environment were those related to the political alignments and activities of the competing core actors related to the High Risk legislation. The existence of unity or divisions within the core actors' ranks on the High Risk issue and/or the extent of their efforts to attract coalition members in support of their positions were viewed as likely to have important consequences for the internal politics and policies of the focal actors.

Data Sources

The data for the study were derived from interviews, archival records, and secondary materials. Telephone and field interviews were conducted with twenty senior staff members affiliated with several organizations. These included the seven focal actors, the U.S. House Subcommittee on Health and Safety, the U.S. Senate Labor Subcommittee (equal numbers of Democratic and Republican staff members), the Occupational Safety and Health Administration (OSHA), the National Association of Manufacturers (NAM), the Business Roundtable, the AFL-CIO, the American Cancer Society (ACS), the American Lung Association (ALA), and the Public Citizen Health Research Group (HRG).

To maximize access to informants and to protect them from possible reprisals, all sources were promised anonymity. This approach was necessitated by the timing and circumstances of the research. Because the legislation was controversial and the research was conducted while the policy-making process was still in motion, virtually none of the informants would agree to talk openly and freely if they were to be identified and quoted. For example, as one source said, "I've had friends fired over this legislation. If you plan to quote me, I'd rather not discuss it."

While anonymous interviewing provides many advantages in terms of generating detailed information (Marshall and Rossman 1989:94), it also presents disadvantages regarding important methodological issues and concerns. For example, the accuracy of the research results is difficult to verify if anonymous interviews constitute the primary sources of information. Readers cannot be sure if anonymity is only a screen to shield respondents or if it is also masking what may be selection biases of the researcher related to choices of respondents and/or the editing of interview content. Another problem is that replication becomes impossible (Shaffir et al. 1980:106). These problems were addressed via a series of procedural compromises and citation practices. First, most informants did agree to be identified on the basis of their organizational affiliations. This provides a meaningful context and frame of reference for most quotes. Second, information derived from anonymous interviews was utilized only when it could be corroborated by at least one other source (either another interview or by archival/secondary materials). Conscientious efforts were made to ensure that wherever possible, corroborating sources were a matter of public record. Finally, equal numbers of supporters and opponents were interviewed.

Primary archival sources consisted of records such as the focal actors' Federal Form 990 tax returns for 1987, congressional subcommittee hearings, reports, prints, and files along with various portions of the *Congressional Record*, Federal Election Commission (FEC) records, and a variety of association proceedings and activities relevant to the legislation as reported in various focal actor publications. Secondary sources included specialty and general publications spanning the 1985-91 period.

Although the number of interviews appears to represent a relatively small sample, two points concerning this issue should be noted. First, the informants were *elites* who, according to the archival research, occupied positions that were most centrally and consistently involved with the High Risk legislation within all organizations considered in the study. Second, *snowball sample* referral questions in the interviews essentially replicated the target list compiled from archival sources. Although the interview list could have extended outward to more peripheral contacts, considerations of the proximity of informants to the High Risk issue along with the realities of limited resources led to a relatively short, but in our view, adequate list.

3

RISK NOTIFICATION: CONCEPT AND POLICY

The most important statement made at all of the [OSHA advisory committee] hearings [on exposures to toxic substances in the workplace] was a statement . . . by Mr. Teplow who represented 50 or 60 of the major chemical manufacturers in this country, in which he challenged the competence of the advisory committee to make recommendations on occupational safety and health. The hearing examiner said to him, "Well Mr. Teplow, how can you do this? You have four top members of industry on the committee." "Ah," said Mr. Teplow, "you misunderstand. These were just scientists. They have no authority or ability to pass judgment on regulatory matters. This is the responsibility of top corporate management and lawyers."

> Testimony of Dr. Samuel S. Epstein, OSHA Congressional Oversight Hearing. U.S. Congress: House, 1974, pp. 196-197.

PRE-OSHA

"Someone Is Stealing Your Life" was the provocative title of a recent essay in *Utne Reader* (Ventura 1991). The author's thesis that most of the value created by our work goes to enrich those who own and control the workplace is both controversial and debatable. However, if the lead had read "Your Work Is Stealing Your Health," many Americans, conditioned by toxic tales from Love Canal (N.Y.) to Bophal (India) to Times Beach (Missouri), would likely be intrigued by such a title. In fact, they would probably want to know more. Survey data indicate that most workers want to know if toxic exposures on the job are putting their health at risk (Noble 1986:124). In short, workers want to be notified if their work is stealing their health.

Risk notification refers to the idea that workers have a right to know whether and/or when they have been exposed to toxic or hazardous substances in the workplace and the extent to which such exposures increase their risks for developing occupationally related diseases (Bayer 1986). The origins of risk notification as a principle and as a program or policy issue both predate and overlap with the OSH Act and are linked to developments in epidemiology, ethics, public policy, and politics.

Epidemiologic studies of workers conducted during the 1960s and 1970s identified numerous groups of workers whose work-related exposures to hazardous substances increased their risks for contracting various occupational diseases, including cancer (e.g., Saffiotti and Wagoner 1976; Selikoff 1976; Selikoff and Hammond 1979; Johnson and Parnes 1979). For the most part, these studies were based upon retrospective cohort methodologies involving comparisons between various types of employment and mortality records. Since these studies did not involve direct, personal contacts with the subjects, health scientists were traditionally not required to obtain informed consent from the subjects in order to conduct the research (Schulte and Ringen 1984).

Once concluded, the results of epidemiologic studies on worker cohorts have usually been made available by the researchers to "employers, employee representatives, and the scientific community" (Schulte and Ringen 1984:485). However, historically and as a matter of policy, occupational health investigators have not been required to notify individual worker-subjects of their research results. This basic arrangement was viewed as ethical and routine, and was essentially unquestioned and unchallenged by most occupational health scientists, employers, workers, and labor unions until approximately the mid-1970s.

During the 1970s, a series of intersecting events and public policy changes related to occupational and environmental health set the stage for a redefinition of traditional ideas and principles regarding the dissemination of epidemiologic research results and risk acceptance by workers. These developments included the emerging environmental movement (Coye et al. 1984:84) and the growth of worker interest in and demands for improvements in workplace health and safety (Donnelly 1982). They also included the passage of various federal statutes related to the first two developments[1] (Schulte and Ringen 1984), and the development of a "right to know" movement (Noble 1986:173-174) among workers as well as "health care providers, lawyers, public health workers, and community activists interested in occupational health" (Coye et al. 1984:94). As a result of these events and circumstances, by the late 1970s and early 1980s, "a major controversy [had] arisen in the media and in the courts over the question of the rights of individual study participants and the public to be notified about epidemiologic study results" (Schulte and Ringen 1984:485).

THE OSH ACT

The enactment of the landmark Occupational Safety and Heath Act (OSH Act) in 1970 was especially important to the emergence and development of risk notification as a policy issue because of the contrast between the principles it enunciated and the ambiguities associated with its implementation. On one hand, the OSH Act explicitly embodied a public policy commitment to "the principle that workers have the right to be protected from workplace hazards" (Schulte and Ringen 1984:485). On the other hand, although the law "provided for the conduct of research on occupational disease . . ., the provisions of the act were not explicit about notifying individuals regarding findings of increased risk of disease associated with occupational exposure" (U.S. Congress: Senate, 1987b:4).

The ethical and political tensions arising from inconsistencies between the expressed principles of the OSH Act, its mandate concerning federal sponsorship of occupational health research, and the law's ambiguous and/or incomplete provisions concerning the dissemination of public-sponsored research results to individual worker-subjects virtually assured that risk notification would quickly emerge in the post-OSHA period as a controversial public health and policy issue. Also, because six of the seven focal actors testified at the OSH Act hearings (only the American Association of Occupational Health Nurses was not represented), and all seven were later involved in various aspects of its implementation, it was virtually certain that these organizations would play a role in the eventual consideration of public policy proposals addressing risk notification as a separate ethical and program issue.

POST-OSHA

The earliest activities related to risk notification following the 1971 implementation of the OSH Act were the result of union-initiated petitions to OSHA for health standards on asbestos. Sheldon Samuels, director for Occupational Safety and Health of the Industrial Union Department (IUD), AFL-CIO, testifying at hearings on occupational disease compensation commented on these early developments: "Within days after the act went into effect, we began working on a petition which was granted for a standard that would provide [our members with] . . . notification [of their exposure to asbestos]" (U.S. Congress: House, 1983:82).

Partly as a result of continuing pressures for action from within organized labor, by the mid 1970s, the National Institute for Occupational Safety and Health (NIOSH) and the National Cancer Institute (NCI) collaborated on the development of two demonstration projects involving risk notification and medical monitoring and intervention for two groups of workers exposed to asbestos and vinyl chloride (U.S. Congress: Senate, 1977:9, 84-85, 99-100).[2] However, as McCaffrey (1982:141) points out:

> These were efforts to pick up the pieces of situations. They involved undeniable health emergencies. No one could deny the necessity for, or lose anything from, government efforts to notify workers whom everyone--including the firms involved--admitted were ill because of workplace chemicals. Also, these were small projects . . . [which] were remedial, noncontroversial,and well within the bounds of current plans, procedures, and resources.

Through contract negotiations and litigation proceedings, labor unions continued to provide much of the impetus for the development of early, post-OSHA efforts involving both individual and more general worker notification projects (Selikoff 1976; Burnham 1977; Noble 1986:184-185; Mendeloff 1988:157). However, risk notification was not widely perceived in the early 1970s as a separate, high priority policy issue within the ranks of organized labor. In the early post-OSHA period, the AFL-CIO and other labor groups were confronted by several more immediate and pressing issues and problems such as the development and enforcement of meaningful health and safety standards in the face of industry hostility to OSHA's efforts in these areas (Coye at al. 1984:86-87).

There is not much doubt that the OSH Act "[awakened] union interest in the issue of [occupational health and safety]" (Donnelly 1982:21); however, at the same time it also united the corporate community and resulted in "a well-funded and well-coordinated campaign against OSHA" (Noble 1986:176-7). The effectiveness of the early industry campaign against the establishment of OSHA health standards for exposure limits to toxic and hazardous substances is apparent by Senator Javits' (R-N.Y.) comment that by 1977, "standards [had] been promulgated for only sixteen substances, and [according to] . . . the General Accounting Office it may take more than a century . . . to establish the needed standards for the other thousands of hazardous substances" (U.S. Congress: Senate, 1977:2). In a later statement, President Carter's Secretary of Labor characterized this situation in these terms: "trying to control carcinogenic substances on a case-by-case basis is like trying to put out a forest fire one tree at a time" (Thompson 1981:239).

STALEMATE AT OSHA

The emerging stalemate at OSHA over the regulation of toxic and hazardous substances in the workplace generated a sense of frustration within organized labor and among the AFL-CIO's political allies in Congress. This sentiment was also shared by sympathetic health professionals within the ranks of OSHA and NIOSH (e.g., U.S. Congress: House, 1974:190-197,235-244,262-283; U.S. Congress: Senate, 1977:1-3, 11-25). Through frustrating, the stalemate also helped trigger increased interest within these same groups in exploring and developing alternative mechanisms and procedures for protecting workers' health--specifically via risk notification. For example, at the 1977 Senate hearings, Senator Schweiker (R-PA) pointed out that he had been working on a bill that would involve NIOSH in risk notification activities:

> I have been working on a bill for some months now that would have utilized NIOSH in the notification of workers who were exposed to hazardous conditions. . . . I found it particularly ironic at the time I was working on the bill to involve NIOSH in notification when a substance is deter-mined to be potentially dangerous to workers, that in fact they had already had situations where hazardous and harmful conditions were known and had not notified workers. I think this hearing is particularly helpful and certainly will have great bearing on my proposal (U.S. Congress: Senate, 1977:3).

Interest among concerned groups in the promotion of risk notification as one kind of policy alternative or supplement to the lengthy, adversarial standard setting process at OSHA was heightened by the accumulation, throughout the 1970s, of research evidence from several sources (including NIOSH) of serious, unchecked, and growing health threats posed to workers as a result of exposures to various toxic substances in numerous occupations (e.g., U.S. Congress: House, 1974; 1975; 1976).[3]

While occupational health activists were not "dormant through the Nixon and Ford years" (Coye et al. 1984:86-87), the political environment of the early to mid-1970s did not provide a context conducive to developing anything more than the previously noted, small-scale emergency and/or demonstration risk notification projects. By contrast, after the election of Jimmy Carter as president in 1976, the political environment shifted in the direction of more support for new and expanded policy directions within both OSHA and NIOSH (including expanded risk notification projects). The appointment of Dr. Eula Bingham as head of OSHA by President Carter "was widely regarded as evidence of a new swing away from the agency's previous pro-industry stance" (Coye et al. 1984:86). Thus, as a result of changes in the political landscape following Carter's election, the stage was set both for the publication and positive political reception of a series of reports and events which would result in the emergence of risk notification as a separate and explicit "major policy issue" (McCaffrey 1982:141).

An important event which helped to initiate this transformation was an April 25, 1977, *New York Times* story: "Agency Lists but Does Not Notify Workers Exposed to Carcinogens" (Burnham 1977:18). The article reported that NIOSH had in its files the names and addresses of "74,000 workers who stand a far greater chance of developing cancer than the general public . . . [and] the head of the institute, Dr. John F. Finklea . . . said further institute studies would probably identify 123,000 more workers who were at risk" (Burnham 1977:18).

The *New York Times* report was quickly followed by a series of related events which collectively helped to elevate risk notification to the level of a high-profile, explicit, and controversial public policy issue. On May 6, 1977, risk notification was the central topic of discussion at a meeting of the National Advisory Committee on Occupational Safety and Health (NACOSH-- another federal government entity created by the OSH Act [McCaffrey 1982:139-141]). On May 9, 1977, the Subcommittee on Labor of the Senate Committee on Human Resources, chaired by Senator Harrison A. Williams (D-N.J.) conducted hearings on "Monitoring of Industrial Workers Exposed to Carcinogens" (U.S. Congress: Senate, 1977). Also, "in July 1977, NIOSH issued the internal document 'The Right to Know: Practical Problems and Policy Issues Arising from Exposure to Hazardous Chemical and Physical Agents in the Workplace'" (Bayer 1986:1353). The NIOSH "right to know" position paper was later appended to the May 9, 1977, Senate Subcommittee on Labor hearing record. This document is important to the development and clarification of risk notification because it represents the first major effort by a federal agency to address the ethical and practical details related to the principle of risk notification and the policy implications of large-scale risk notification programs.

Insofar as ethical principles related to risk notification were concerned, the NIOSH paper asserted that "Clearly workers have a right to know whether or not they are exposed to hazardous chemical and physical agents regulated by the Federal Government." It also added a caveat: "However, this right is linked to a complex series of problems which must be faced and resolved if any worker notification program is to be successful" (U.S. Congress: Senate, 1977:44). In terms of size, scope, and expense, the report estimated the costs of individually notifying some 21 million workers exposed to hazardous substances at approximately $40 million and the "total program costs [were]

. . . estimated to be $54 billion" (U.S. Congress: Senate, 1977: 74, 71). The latter figure includes the costs of lifetime medical surveillance for those workers who would require such services. In essence, "The 'Right to Know' position paper basically said this to Congress: 'Here's what you're getting into if we do this. Now do you REALLY want us to go ahead?'" (original emphasis, McCaffrey 1982:145).

THE 1977-1980 PERIOD

As Bayer (1986:1353) points out, "The flurry of concern initiated by the *Times* expose and the Senate hearings had spent itself [by the end of 1977]. With the exception of a small number of representatives of organized labor, almost no one pressured NIOSH to move forward expeditiously." This interpretation of the status and priority of risk notification as a policy issue in the post-1977 period was reinforced in an interview with a senior AFL-CIO staff member: "The labor movement got more involved at that point in time but not in a major way; there was some interest in working with NIOSH and other agencies to develop additional pilot programs on risk notification."

During the 1978-81 period three major pilot notification programs were "initiated through the efforts of NIOSH, the National Cancer Institute, and worker organizations" (U.S. Congress: Senate, 1987b:10). These programs represented important collaborative efforts involving labor, government, and industry to extend and refine the notification activities and principles developed in earlier notification efforts (Schulte and Ringen 1984:486-487). The notification projects involved three cohorts of different sizes and with different suspected carcinogens. The Augusta, Georgia, group involved 1,150 (70 percent black male) workers suspected of exposure to Beta-naphthylamine, which may cause bladder cancer. A second group, nationwide in distribution, consisted of 10,000 currently and 2,000 formerly employed white male "pattern makers" suspected of exposure to unknown carcinogens with an increased risk of colon-rectal cancer. The third group was comprised of Port Allegany, Pennsylvania, Flint Glass Workers; it involved 1,200 white male workers suspected of exposure to asbestos, which may cause various respiratory cancers (Schulte and Ringen 1984:489). Together, these three projects involved the notification of approximately 14,000 workers of their increased risks for contracting occupationally related diseases. The projects also included provisions which encouraged and/or enabled notified workers to seek medical monitoring and counseling services (Schulte and Ringen 1984:488-489; U.S. Congress: Senate, 1987b:10-11).

THE EARLY 1980s

The initiation of the demonstration projects coincided with the emergence of a new political climate that was generally less favorable to increased activities in support of workers' health and safety than the conditions which had prevailed during the late 1970s. The 1980 election of Ronald Reagan as president and a Republican majority in the U.S. Senate (which was maintained until the 1986 elections) signaled the beginning of what would be a difficult decade for organized labor. The general, antilabor tone which came to pervade this period was initiated when the Reagan administration fired striking air traffic controllers in August 1981. This action eliminated 80 percent of the 15,000 controllers employed by the Federal Aviation Administration (FAA) and also resulted in the dissolution of their "union" known as the Professional Air Traffic Controllers Organization (PATCO)[4] (Tesh 1988:108-109). Following the administration's destruction of PATCO, organized labor found itself on the defensive on a wide range of issues including not only health and safety, but also on critical economic and membership issues such as concessions bargaining and plant closings. To make matters worse, the early antilabor actions of the Reagan presidency transpired in the context of "the worst recession that this nation [had] seen since the 1930s" (Tillett et al. 1986:725).

As a consequence--at least in part--of these conditions, efforts by federal agencies to expand risk notification programs came to a virtual standstill. At the same time risk notification as a policy priority was temporarily relegated by the leadership of organized labor to what one informant characterized as a "back-burner position." However, in the midst of these unfavorable trends and events, support for risk notification persisted--especially among some senior AFL-CIO staff members, some members of Congress, and among concerned health professionals within NIOSH and OSHA. Thus, "by mid-1981, frustration on the part of advocates of notification resulted in yet another decision to call upon the press. On this occasion, staff of the Workers Institute for Safety and Health (WISH) and some within NIOSH turned to *The Washington Post*" (Bayer 1986:1353). At the same time, media attention at the regional level also helped to stimulate public and political interest in risk notification during 1981 and 1982 (Schulte et al. 1985:25).

Efforts by supporters of risk notification to reposition it as a high profile policy issue led to an August 24, 1981, front-page story in the *Washington Post*: "Millions Not Told of Job Health Perils" (Omang 1981). The article described the Augusta, Georgia, demonstration notification project and went on to point out that "NIOSH officials estimate that their lists alone, which detail only places later found to involve carcinogens, include about 200,000 names" (Omang 1981:1). Following publication of the *Post* story, health professionals within NIOSH who were concerned with the protection of workers' health began to press once again for internal agency policies which would lead to involving NIOSH in larger and more comprehensive worker notification projects (Bayer 1986:1353-1354).

Parallel to these developments within NIOSH, organized labor began to devote more of its resources to the notification issue:

> The AFL-CIO . . .launched . . . a major new drive to deal with worker health problems. "There has to be exposure notification," said Joe Velasquez, director of the Workers' Institute [for Safety and Health]. "Society has the responsibility to take care of these people. It's blaming the victim to say the worker has to take care of himself" (Omang 1981:A-5).

In the period following the *Post* article, the higher priority which the AFL-CIO leadership (as encouraged by some senior staff members) assigned to risk notification as a major public policy and legislative issue was evident in the organization's legislative agenda. Working with Democratic members of the House, the AFL-CIO strongly supported legislation introduced in 1982 (Occupational Health Hazards Compensation Act, H.R. 5735) and 1983 (Occupational Disease Compensation Act, H.R. 3175) directed at reforming the workers' compensation system. The purpose of the legislation was to more fairly and adequately compensate the victims of occupational diseases. Congressman George Miller (D-Calif.), as Chairman of the House Subcommittee on Labor Standards, helped move the labor policy initiative forward. In his opening remarks in support of H.R. 5735 in 1982, Congressman Miller described the state of workers' compensation in the United States as it related to victims of occupational diseases:

> The present compensation system is simply not designed for occupational diseases. Instead the system takes workers who are victims of . . . disabling or fatal diseases due to their jobs and makes them victims again--victims of an indifferent system which denies them, their families, and their survivors the income maintenance and the medical care which they need and to which they are fully entitled. This committee has spent some 8 years looking into this problem. . . . It is time, I think, to end the debate that has gone on over that time (U.S. Congress: House, 1982:1).

The 1982 and 1983 House bills addressing this issue included several provisions that essentially combined risk notification with eligibility for occupationally induced disease compensation.

As a result of opposition from within the corporate sector, especially the insurance industry, the 1982 and 1983 bills never moved beyond the initial hearings held by the Labor Standards Subcommittee. Even so, the bills provided a preview of many important features that would later be incorporated into the High Risk bills. These included (for example) legal proscriptions disallowing employer discrimination against employees identified as potentially afflicted by occupational diseases, the 30 percent notification "trigger," and the concept of an expert "advisory committee" made up of appointed medical scientists to review occupational health research in order to identify groups of workers at risk of being afflicted by occupational diseases (U.S. Congress: House, 1982:47-53). Although the bills were never voted on in the House, the willingness of the AFL-CIO leadership to testify and commit significant organizational resources to secure the basic notification features in the bills underscored the high priority that organized labor had come to assign to risk notification as a public policy issue in the early 1980s.

After the 1983 hearings on H.R. 3175, senior staff members within the AFL-CIO's Industrial Union Department (IUD) developed and began to circulate to member unions a draft proposal for a bill that would address risk notification as a separate piece of legislation. As one AFL-CIO official said in an interview, "We decided that rather than trying to reform the workers' compensation system--which we've been trying to do for 20 years--we would concentrate on a risk notification bill." The efforts on behalf of risk notification within the IUD unfolded over 1983-84 and intersected with, and were related to, several other important events which helped to crystallize congressional, media, and public interest in risk notification legislation.

1984 AS A TURNING POINT

Events favorable to the IUD's efforts to develop and win political support for risk notification legislation actually began to break in late 1983. In November, OSHA issued the Hazard Communication Standard[5] which, as interview sources indicated, not only reiterated the "right to know" principle but also "increased the visibility and political possibilities for risk notification." Early in 1984, reports and information from the three pilot demonstration projects began to circulate stating that risk notification was both practical and feasible (Schulte and Ringen 1984).

Within the first half of 1984, NIOSH-based advocates of risk notification succeeded in overcoming internal agency sentiments against the expansion of

NIOSH-sponsored risk notification projects. In spite of a lack of enthusiasm for enlarging the agency's notification activities by the Reagan-appointed director (Dr. J. Donald Millar), in mid-1984, NIOSH, in conjunction with the Centers for Disease Control (CDC) forwarded "to [the] [D]HHS [Department of Health and Human Services] a request for $4 million to begin the process of notifying 25,000 workers in five cohorts" (Bayer 1986:1355). However, this funding request was denied by DHHS and led directly to a major press announcement by Ralph Nader and Dr. Sidney Wolfe (the Director of Public Citizen's Health Research Group) on October 22, 1984. They stated in part that:

> NIOSH had in its files the names of between 200,000 and 250,000 workers "who have been identified in sixty-six studies [and who] have never been individually notified that they may have faced an increased probability of contracting cancer or other illnesses from exposure to dangerous workplace chemicals" (Bayer 1986:1352).

The Public Citizen announcement was quickly followed by a *New York Times* editorial on November 2, 1984: "Keeping Ill Workers in Ignorance." The editorial criticized NIOSH for not notifying workers exposed to hazardous substances of their increased risks for developing cancer. It went on to cite political considerations and motives as central to the failure of NIOSH to take action and it endorsed risk notification as a matter of policy on the grounds of ethics and as a cost-prevention measure (*New York Times* 1984:A26).

Subsequent to the *Times* editorial, the 1984 elections resulted in Reagan's reelection, but the outcomes at the congressional level produced a distribution of House and Senate seats more favorable to the Democrats and to proponents of risk notification. Despite the fact that Republicans retained a majority in the Senate after the 1984 elections, several informants cited the results as important in creating a political climate where risk notification legislation would receive a much more favorable hearing. As a senior congressional staff member stated: "There was a lot of feeling in Congress that because of the way the election went in 1984 that the country was tired of this deregulation emphasis of Ronald Reagan and now we could begin to pass new initiatives again and that's why I think [the High Risk legislation] came up in 1985."

The view that the political climate played an important role in the timing of the introduction of the High Risk legislation was shared by some of the witnesses at the hearings on H.R. 1309. For example, in a personal reflection on the changes leading to reform in this area, Dr. Kenneth B. Miller, occupational health physician for the Oil, Chemical and Atomic Workers

International Union, stated in the 1985 congressional hearings: "I think the tide is turning on these issues because people are being affected . . . I think it is the strongest rising political issue that is out there among people that, yes it is overtaking Congress" (U.S. Congress: House, 1985:211).

4

HIGH RISK
LEGISLATION: 1985-88

This is the most important occupational health legislation of
the past decade. . . . A vote against this bill is a vote for the
high-paid and well-heeled lobbyists who are doing so much
to try to defeat the legislation. . . .The high-priced lobbyists
conceivably can prevail. If they prevail, they will make their
dollars, but it is the people of this country that will suffer.
> Senator Howard Metzenbaum [D-Ohio],*Congression-
> al Record*, 1988a, p. S2767; 1988b, pp. S3179, S3162.

This is another do-good, costly, unworkable, liberal spending
bill. . . . We all know why people are voting for and against
this bill; it is because of political pressure, as far as I can see
it. . . . I have not seen an overwhelming vote for this yet nor
have I seen a majority vote for it. I am sure that if the truth
was known and this was a secret ballot, this bill would not
get more than 25 votes.
> Senator Orrin Hatch [R-Utah], *Congressional Record*,
> 1988b, pp. S3153, S3163.

The long screw of history is still turning.
> Hunter S. Thompson, *Generation of Swine*. 1988,
> p. 50.

DEVELOPMENT OF H.R. 1309

Long-time advocates of risk notification in and out of the labor movement had
watched for and helped to put in place the propitious events and circumstances which, in late 1984 and early 1985, presented an opportunity for a realistic
and serious political reception for the High Risk legislation. By early 1985,

labor-based advocates of risk notification had succeeded in lining up both internal and external political and organizational support for a major legislative push on risk notification. At this time, "the [high risk] legislation . . . [was] a top priority of organized labor" (Matlack 1987:832).

The high priority which labor assigned to this issue reflected both a genuine concern for workers' health and a recognition that since it could be presented as a public health issue, its chances for success were increased. If it were to succeed, such an outcome would not only provide increased protection for workers' health, but also serve as an opening wedge for improving the chances for action on other items on labor's legislative agenda. The business press characterized this situation in similar terms: "The measure [was] at the forefront of labor unions' attempts to revive a spate of bills that [were] aimed at improving worker wages or conditions and that [had] been stagnant through most of the Reagan administration" (Karr 1987:59).

The draft of the first High Risk bill was a variation of the IUD document which had been circulated in 1983. As one union staff member closely involved with the development of the initial bill reported: "By 1985 senior staff members from IUD had got (sic) together with some of the most respected health scientists who had been long-time advocates of a risk notification program and sat down with the principals of the two committees and developed the first high risk bill." Their hope was that their actions would help put an end to "15 years of conflicting policies and inaction" (U.S. Congress: Senate, 1987b:4).

On February 27, 1985, the High Risk legislation was introduced in the U.S. House by Representatives Joseph M. Gaydos (D-PA) and Augustus F. Hawkins (D-Calif.) as H.R. 1309. The purpose of the bill was to develop a procedure for notifying workers whose jobs increased their risks for developing occupational diseases and to provide such "at risk" workers with medical monitoring to facilitate secondary disease prevention via job transfers and medical intervention (*Congressional Record* 1985:H816). As initially drafted, H.R. 1309 provided for the creation of a five-member "Risk Assessment Board" within NIOSH. The board would review scientific studies related to the occurrence of occupational diseases and recommend to the secretary of Health and Human Services (HHS) that workers in populations exposed to conditions which resulted in a 30 percent higher rate[1] of occupational diseases than in nonexposed worker populations be notified of their elevated risk status.

H.R. 1309 resulted in five days of hearings before the House subcommittees on Health and Safety and Labor Standards over the period from October 9, 1985, to March 19, 1986. It provoked an immediate and virtually total polarization among business and labor groups. The bill was opposed by all of the core actors within the business community including ten major trade associations and business federations (e.g., NAM, the Chemical Manufacturers

Association (CMA) the American Insurance Association (AIA), and the U.S. Chamber of Commerce). These groups testifying against the legislation had a total corporate membership of over 200,000 (U.S. Congress: House, 1985; Morehouse 1988a). The full extent of corporate opposition also extended to dozens of smaller trade associations and thousands of individual corporations. Among organized labor, the legislation was actively supported by the AFL-CIO as well as by at least thirty nine large individual unions. These included not only unions based in manufacturing and mining such as the United Auto Workers (UAW), Oil, Chemical and Atomic Workers (OCAW), United Steel Workers of America (USWA), and the United Mine Workers (UMW), but also service and public sector unions such as the Service Employees International Union (SEIU), and the American Federation of State, County, and Municipal Employees (AFSCME) (U.S. Congress: House 1985-88). The bill was also supported by some professional societies and health organizations (including the American Association of Occupational Health Nurses, the American Public Health Association, the American Psychological Association, and the American Lung Association) and citizens' groups such as Public Citizen and the Health Research Group. It was also opposed by one professional association, the American Industrial Hygiene Association.

The sharp tone of the political conflicts over the legislation was registered and reflected in the hearings testimony where business and labor representatives' remarks were frequently laced with pejorative terms (e.g., "phony, political, ill-conceived, misrepresentation, and bad science") aimed at discrediting each others' motives and views on the legislation (U.S. Congress: House, 1985). In interviews, many informants made statements echoing the sentiments expressed by two congressional staff members on the tone of the political battles over the legislation. One noted "This was one of the most bruising fights I've seen in my career and I've been here a long time." Another informant said "The battles over this [legislation] involved real political hardball; I mean labor aggressively supported the bill, but the business community went absolutely crazy in opposing it. I've never seen anything like it." These sharp divisions and conflicts between the positions of business and labor on H.R. 1309 indicated that both sides understood that the stakes were high in terms of the legislation's potential redistributive consequences at the economic and ideological and/or political levels.

ECONOMIC REDISTRIBUTIVE EFFECTS: THE BUSINESS PERSPECTIVE

Testimony presented by all members of the business community during the 1985-87 House and Senate hearings illustrated a clear, class-like interpretation of the economic redistributive potential of the High Risk Act. For example, NAM (which includes approximately 13,000 corporate members and which led business opposition to the bills) representatives testified that if the High Risk bills were to pass, "the business community can expect at least $112 billion in litigation claims in the first year of the program" (U.S. Congress: House, 1987a:400). Aside from the potential litigation costs, corporate opponents were also concerned about the costs of providing medical monitoring and testing services to notified employees. According to a report commissioned by opponents of the legislation and prepared by Robert R. Nathan Associates, Inc. (a Washington, D.C., based consulting firm), "Direct costs are estimated to reach $119 million per year" (*Congressional Record* 1988c:S3231). In summarizing the economic basis for business opposition to the legislation based upon its potential redistributive implications, one source based in a health association in the Washington, D.C., policy-making community observed: "industry was opposed to the legislation because they knew it was going to be costly for them; they just didn't know how many zeroes would be involved."

ECONOMIC REDISTRIBUTIVE EFFECTS: THE LABOR PERSPECTIVE

The view among labor supporters of the legislation was, in the words of one union staff member, that some firms had long been "getting away with murder" and if the bill redistributed some health-related costs to businesses and provided workers with greater economic security that was viewed as a "reasonable outcome." A similar perspective was also reflected in the 1985 hearings as Margaret Seminario, testifying on behalf of the AFL-CIO stated, "I think . . . this bill may result in more compensation claims and suits against product manufacturers [but] . . . what we need to establish in this country is a system for the compensation of individuals who suffer from occupational diseases" (U.S. Congress: House, 1985:199). The gross undercompensation of the victims of occupational diseases and the legitimacy of redistributing some corporate resources to support workers victimized by occupationally induced diseases were noted by Dr. Kenneth B. Miller testifying on behalf of the Oil, Chemical and Atomic Workers: "In 1980 . . . only 5 percent of people who have occupational diseases actually receive any compensation from the workers' compensation system. . . . This bill would greatly assist such individuals [who now receive no compensation]" (Ibid:192-193). Labor representatives understood that in the long term the High Risk Act would lead to more studies regarding occupational health. It would serve the dual purpose of promoting more primary prevention efforts as more information was generated and at the same time aid in legitimizing workers' compensation claims based upon occupational disease disabilities. As Dr. Miller observed, "[This bill would have a] multiplier effect . . . in terms of increasing the awareness of occupational disease among workers, their physicians, and all those who would be involved in the spinoff research projects which would develop from such notification programs" (Ibid:196).

While union representatives acknowledged that the legislation might effect the redistribution of some corporate economic resources towards protecting workers' health and economic security, they disagreed with what they saw as a gross exaggeration by the business community of the amounts of money involved. Labor supporters asserted that the Georgia case, which had been used as the basis for industry estimates of litigation claims, was atypical and could not serve as a legitimate basis for extrapolating possible litigation costs. It involved a chemical (Beta-napthylamine) that had been known to cause cancer since the 1930s and had been banned from use in several European countries since the 1950s. Of the 1,150 workers notified of their increased risks for bladder cancer, 171 lawsuits were filed but most were settled out of court for a total amount of approximately $500,000 (U.S. Congress: Senate, 1987b:15-16). As more typical of the likely litigation consequences of risk notification, labor pointed to two other NIOSH pilot studies which had produced very few lawsuits (Ibid:15). At the same time, the validity of the corporate-financed Nathan study estimate of medical monitoring costs were also challenged by labor since the Senate Committee on Labor and Human Resources Report estimated annual direct costs to industry as "between $7.4 and $22.3 million" (Ibid:15).

In short, the business view was that the cost implications of the legislation would be so extreme as to constitute an unfair burden upon corporations. Labor's interpretation was that the costs would be both modest and any redistributive effects would be fair. For both sides these contradictory interpretations rested on very different assumptions regarding the bills' effects and what constituted a fair and just division of economic resources among business and labor.

IDEOLOGICAL AND POLITICAL REDISTRIBUTIVE EFFECTS

Beyond the publicly debated cost issues, the potential redistributive effects of the High Risk Act at the ideological and political levels were equally, if not more, important in energizing the political conflicts between labor and business over the legislation. While this dimension of the struggles over the bills was never *publicly* cited by the participants or explicitly reported by the media as a point of contention, it surfaced repeatedly in interviews as a critical issue--especially as an important factor underlying business opposition to the legislation. One senior congressional staff member acknowledged the importance of this factor and bluntly stated that "A lot of business opposition was ideological. There is a sense in the business community--'Hey, just leave us alone and we'll take care of what has to be done'. . . [but] you can't do it voluntarily. It won't be done. You have to have a mandate." Like the OSH Act before it, the corporate community perceived the High Risk legislation as a significant political threat to its ideological and political interests. In symbolic politics terms, the act was viewed by industry as likely to curtail corporate autonomy and also generate ideological and/or political empowering effects for workers. One source with high-level political and industry contacts commenting on corporate concerns with the potential ideological/political redistributive aspects of the legislation pointedly observed:

> A decision was made involving top corporate officials and the White House that they could not let the labor agenda be passed by the [100th] Congress. That included things like mandated health benefits [for workers] and this [High Risk Act] was one of the main bills, and by God they had to stop it no matter what the cost. To not stop the bill would send the wrong signal to labor and would be costly for business in more ways than one.

This observation illustrates the very real business concern that if the legislation was passed, it would send a signal that labor was alive and moving back in the direction of political potency--exactly the opposite of what business had been working to achieve through the Reagan administration. This view of corporate opposition to the High Risk Act as linked to ideological and political factors represents a logical extension of what is known about business opposition to OSHA. Calavita (1983), Szasz (1984), and Noble (1986) have documented the powerful, coordinated, and effective corporate campaigns of the 1970s and early 1980s aimed at "gutting" OHSA's effectiveness and "delegitimizing" the agency insofar as it symbolically represented state legitimation of workers' concern for occupational health and safety. The corporate campaigns also limited OSHA's effectiveness as a potential source of political power for legitimizing labor's political agenda in areas outside of occupational safety and health.

Although many labor supporters of the legislation recognized ideology as an important basis for business opposition, it was seldom mentioned in interviews as relevant to labor's reasons for supporting its passage. For the most part, union sources emphasized the practical economic and health benefits for workers rather than the collective, ideological and/or political-power redistributive consequences that might attend the passage of the legislation. However, while labor supporters did not frame their support for the legislation on the basis of explicit ideological or political objectives, their motives were perceived as including such considerations by other members of the policy-making community. A staff member of a health association expressed a common sentiment among non-labor supporters of the bills:

> In a sense we were being used--and we knew it. Labor saw the High Risk Act as a way of jump-starting their broader agenda. After being hammered by the Reagan administration for five years, they needed a win. By painting High Risk as a public health, anti-cancer bill, they thought they would have a good chance to get moving again.

PROFESSIONAL SOCIETIES
AND THE POLICY PROCESS

Representatives from core actor organizations linked to both business and labor indicated that they actively sought to enlist health and safety professional associations in support of their positions on the legislation. Interview sources also reported that similar activities were undertaken by the staff of congressmen and senators who were active supporters and opponents of the legislation. A congressional staff member opposed to the legislation characterized the situation in these terms:

> What happens is that both sides of an issue--the proponents and opponents--the proponents will go around and try and coerce the [professional associations] to support the legislation. The opponents are going around to the same groups trying to get them either to not support it or at the very least, not to take a position. So that's kind of how these things in reality happen.

Supporters and opponents of the legislation agreed that the professional societies had the potential to legitimize their respective positions with their "scientific expertise," and thus could be influential in mobilizing additional political support for which ever position they supported. One representative of a trade association opposed to the legislation acknowledged the reality and the importance of recruiting professional association support in the High Risk case:

> We were always trying to get the health associations on our
> side. I think they were perceived as kind of wearing the
> "white hats" and not so likely to have a kind of hidden
> political agenda. I always hated to follow them in lobby visits
> because they always had the better arguments. In this debate
> at least I think they carried a lot of clout and depending on
> what side they were on--I mean it did make a difference. So
> we made a lot of efforts to try and get them on our side.

A similar view was echoed by a political opponent of the legislation in the
Congress:

> They're not lobby groups, but they are professionals. And so,
> it's always important in a debate to have them on your side
> because if all of the health professionals are on the other
> side, it's difficult for me to point to any valid reasons [for
> opposing the legislation] other than pure politics.

As the political struggles on the High Risk bills began to unfold, many of
the professional associations did become involved--often taking positions that
were perceived by core actor representatives to be linked to their economic
interests and/or interorganizational linkages.   For example, an AFL-CIO-
based supporter of the legislation maintained that the positions of silence and
opposition (of the American Occupational Medical Association and American
Industrial Hygiene Association respectively) were understandable because the
former organization was "dominated by company doctors" and the latter
organization was composed of "mostly corporate guys."   An opponent of the
legislation based in a professional association took a cynical view towards the
support of the AAOHN for the legislation: "As long as the legislation had a
role for occupational health nurses, they'd support it."

Aside from the focal actors, two health groups that were not strictly
professional associations were repeatedly characterized by supporters and
opponents of the legislation as *the* most vigorous proponents of the bills within
the health community: The American Lung Association and the American
Cancer Society. The American Lung Association was an early supporter of
H.R. 1309 (and the later bills) and the American Cancer Society became
actively involved with the bills in the 1987-88 period. As supporters of the
legislation, both of these organizations, like some of the supporting professional societies, found themselves under pressure from opponents to either change
their positions or at least become neutral. As one Congressional source
stated: "these groups could have buckled; they were under crude, crude
pressures [from the opposition] and they could have buckled but they didn't."

It is apparent that both sides saw the professional societies and the other health groups as important resources in the struggles over the High Risk legislation. It is also clear that interorganizational linkages of the sort which this inquiry addresses, as well as politically based incentives and sanctions, were utilized by both sides in efforts to mobilize the "scientific support" which these groups represented for their positions. Thus, among the core actor groups, efforts to get the health and safety associations and other health groups involved as allies or at least to keep them neutral were early and continuing concerns for both sides.

THE POLITICAL CONTEXT AND HIGH RISK BILLS AFTER 1985

H.R. 1309 was amended in mid-1986 but by the end of the year it had not been voted on by the House Health and Safety Subcommittee. Despite this lack of movement and the initial, sharply conflicting positions of labor and business towards the legislation, shifting events and circumstances during 1986 and 1987 helped set the stage for the emergence of some common ground and efforts to work out a business-labor compromise on the issue. The 1986 elections resulted in the Democrats regaining control of the Senate and, thus, enhanced the political prospects for the High Risk legislation. At the same time, organized labor was increasing successful in defining the High Risk bills in public health terms. For example, by early 1987 a Reagan-appointed Labor Department official commented that the legislation was "difficult to oppose . . . [because] it had been seen as [an anti] 'cancer bill'" (Karr 1987:59). It was in the context of these and other events that the High Risk legislation was introduced once again in early 1987.

1987: New Context, New High Risk Bills

As the 100th Congress opened under a new set of political conditions, the High Risk legislation was introduced during the first week of January 1987 in the House as H.R. 162 and also in the Senate (for the first time) as S.79. Hearings were held on the bills by both the House Subcommittee on Health and Safety and the Senate Subcommittee on Labor during February, March, and early April of 1987. The turning point, which considerably brightened the political prospects for the legislation, resulted from the interplay between shifting political circumstances and varying interests and priorities within the corporate sector in late 1986 and early 1987. According to various informants, in early 1987 a series of negotiations were conducted involving primarily

Senator Metzenbaum and his staff, senior staff members from organized labor, and representatives from a variety of industry trade associations as well as from individual corporations.   At these meetings the Senate and House sponsors of the legislation, with the advice and consent of organized labor, agreed to several major changes in the legislation. These mutually-agreed upon changes were part of a *quid pro quo* arrangement which resulted in significant, public business support for the High Risk bills in the 100th Congress.

As a result of these negotiations and other compromise changes added later as the bills moved through the House and into the Senate, the legislation was modified in several areas. Of particular importance were agreements to modify six key provisions of the bills.

1. Risk Assessment Board Size. It would be expanded from five to either seven or nine members.

2. Litigation Limitations. Provisions were added that explicitly prohibited workers from using notifications as the basis for tort claims against employers or as the basis for "stress claims" (i.e., lawsuits based upon claims of emotional fears and psychological harm resulting from notifications).

3. Basis for Notification. Only human studies could be used as the basis for notification. The 30 percent "trigger" notification requirement was dropped in favor of more judgmental discretion on the part of the Risk Assessment Board insofar as the criteria which they would utilize in assessing causal linkages between exposures and occupational diseases and which would lead to notification.

4. Limitations and Exemptions. Employers who could show that because of mitigating factors in the workplace which modified risks to otherwise notified workers could be exempt from procedures requiring medical monitoring and possible medical removal; also, small businesses (under 100 employees) and employers of seasonal agricultural workers were generally to be exempt from the medical removal provisions of the legislation.

5. Medical Monitoring Costs "Cap." Medical monitoring costs of employers of fifty or fewer workers would be limited to no more than $250 per year (to be adjusted for inflation in later years).

6. Physician Liability. Physicians would be protected from malpractice suits that might be brought against them as a result of "good faith" decisions which they might make as part of the medical monitoring and medical transfer/removal provisions of the bills (U.S. Congress: Senate, 1987b).

High Risk Corporate Support

The 1987 subcommittee hearings testimony on H.R. 162 and S.79 are instructive in many ways in terms of understanding the development of the High Risk legislation. However, taken alone, the hearings do not reflect the behind-the-scenes negotiations and nor do they reflect emerging support for the High Risk bills among important segments of the business community. For example, the Chemical Manufacturers Association (CMA), one of the important trade groups which eventually supported the legislation, was represented at both the Senate and House hearings in the spring of 1987. In both instances, the organization continued to express public opposition to the legislation. In a prepared statement to the Senate subcommittee on March 9, 1987, the CMA's position stated: "In its present form, . . . S.79 does not provide a sound basis for . . . informing workers of significant health risks in the workplace" (U.S. Congress: Senate, 1987a:209). Two weeks later (on March 24), George Rodenhausen represented the CMA at the House hearings and testified against H.R. 162 (which was nearly identical to S.79): "Mr. Gaydos: 'You are against the bill?' Mr. Rodenhausen: 'We are currently opposed to the bill.'" (U.S. Congress: House, 1987a:200). Despite these expressions of opposition, two weeks after the House testimony (on April 8, 1987), the CMA sent a letter signed by the association's President (Mr. Robert A. Roland) to Senator Metzenbaum. The letter thanked the senator for the opportunity to participate in the negotiations concerning changes in the bill and expressed the organization's support for S.79 (U.S. Congress: Senate, 1987c:26).

The example of the CMA's seeming inconsistency towards the legislation was repeated several times for other corporate organizations as the off-the-record negotiations produced significant business support for the bills. The result was that despite universally negative testimony by corporations and trade associations in early 1987, by mid-to-late spring, the House and Senate subcommittees began circulating nearly identical lists of twenty nine business organizations that had expressed public support for the legislation in letters to the subcommittees[2] (U.S. Congress: House, 1985-88; Senate, 1986-1988).[3] The lists included as supporters of the revised versions of H.R. 162 and S.79 a limited but important segment of the business community including the CMA (170 member companies), the American Electronics Association (AEA--3,200 member companies), and the National Paint and Coatings Association (NPCA--1,000+ member companies) as well as twenty six large, individual corporations such as ARCO, Ciba-Geigy, Union Carbide, Eastman Kodak, Digital Equipment Corporation, IBM, and General Electric. In addition to the lists, the House and Senate subcommittees also had letters on file from most of these organizations expressing their support for the revised versions of the bills.

The Basis of Business Support

According to informants on both sides of the issue, the reasons underlying the decision of business supporters to break ranks with the majority of businesses and trade associations on the High Risk bills were linked to a rewards-costs interpretation. That is, leaders in policy-setting positions within the supportive corporations and trade associations reportedly became convinced that by agreeing to support substantially revised versions of the High Risk bills, they and their organizations would gain more than they might lose. Adding to this view was a sense of uncertainty which existed in early 1987; the prospect existed that the bills might pass in spite of corporate opposition and, thus, would include few, if any provisions favorable to their interests and perhaps many provisions unfavorable to their interests. In short, as one source put it: "the revised bills they were able to get had more pluses than minuses for the group."

This rewards-costs interpretation was a recurring theme in many interviews and was explicitly applied to at least three specific areas where corporate supporters shared some common, practical concerns which they saw as an opportunity to address with the High Risk bills: (1) liability protection and limitations, (2) public relations and image issues (especially among chemical companies), (3) realistic evaluations of anticipated impacts and effects of the legislation upon corporate operations and profits.

Several sources pointed out that the issue of liability protection has long been an important area of concern for the business community. Over the years there have been numerous corporate-sponsored efforts to pass federal legislation that would restrict tort claims and product liability suits brought against corporations by workers and/or consumers. For the most part though, these efforts have not been successful. As one senior congressional staff member observed: "There's never gonna be a federal product liability law or tort reform legislation the way these [corporate] guys want it."

Within the context of corporate interest in liability protection legislation and the reality that such reforms were politically unlikely, some corporations and trade associations reportedly saw in the High Risk bills a relatively "inexpensive" (in terms of a cost-benefit perspective) opportunity to achieve some significant reforms and protections in this area. Both labor and supportive corporate sources indicated that each side stood to gain from the compromises made on the legislation. Since the negotiated revisions of the High Risk bills were supported by organized labor, by Ralph Nader's organizations, and by the American trial lawyers, supportive corporations could get an important measure of protection from worker liability claims without major political conflicts. Also, because the revised bills included language that preempted stress claims based on the notification of workers under state laws, there would be greater uniformity and less uncertainty for corporations with the states removed from the picture on this issue.

Those corporations and trade associations that essentially traded their support for the High Risk bills in return for concessions in the areas of liability and litigation limitations were confident that the revised bills adequately and expertly addressed their concerns.[4] As congressional sources pointed out, this sense of assurance derived from the fact that a corporate lobbyist with expertise in these areas assisted in drafting the liability limitations sections of the revised High Risk bills. At the time, this attorney was a senior member of the corporate Product Liability Reform effort; since then, he has moved on to a similar senior position with the American Tort Reform effort. Evidence of the satisfaction among corporate supporters of the revised bills concerning the liability issue is illustrated in a letter from Crum & Forster Insurance Companies (a corporate supporter of the legislation) addressed to Senator Hollings (D-SC) as part of an unsuccessful effort to win his support for S.79; Senior Vice President Leslie Cheek wrote the following on March 22, 1988:

> We are supporting S.79 because we think it will improve our
> ability, as workers' compensation and general liability carriers,
> to prevent harm that gives rise to claims in these lines of
> insurance. In our view, enactment of the legislation will
> improve the insurability of employers in affected industries
> (U.S. Congress: Senate 1986-88).[5]

A second specific concern of corporate organizations willing to support the High Risk bills involved the issues of image and public relations. Several interview sources indicated that many companies within the chemical industry had a strong interest in being able to support legislation of a positive sort to boost their public image and enhance their legitimacy in the aftermath of numerous negative press reports concerning the health effects of toxic chemicals in both the workplace and community environments.[6] This was especially important to them as opinion polls continued to show strong public fears of cancers related to chemical exposures, distrust of chemical companies to regulate themselves, and support for government regulation of toxic chemicals (Noble 1986:124). In recounting the reasons for industry support for the High Risk bills, one former trade association official bluntly stated, "First of all there was an image issue. I think the chemical industry especially wanted to be for something in the environmental area given their mistakes and the way that people perceived them."

With regard to the issue of the anticipated impact of the legislation upon corporate operations and profits, many sources suggested that at least a few of the corporations supporting the legislation were doing so because, for a variety of reasons, they expected to be unaffected by it. This motive was linked to the public relations angle in that supportive companies would receive "positive image points" by appearing to be the "white hats" (terms used by informants) without being affected because, in many cases, they already had programs in place for monitoring and/or protecting workers' health which would exempt them under the variance provisions of the revised bills. Additional evidence for the interpretation that at least some corporate support was grounded in the expectation that the legislation would not affect their operations is provided by an observation by then Senator Quayle (R-Ind.) during the Senate debates on S.79:

> We [who oppose S.79] have serious questions about the value
> of support from a group that is not going to be affected by
> the legislation. I mean, it is pretty easy to go ahead and
> support the legislation if you do not think you are going to
> be affected by it. . . . Most [companies which support S.79],
> it appears, are not affected by it (*Congressional Record*
> 1988a:S2782-2783).

Although the exact mix of motives underlying the emergence of business support is complex and difficult to know with certainty,[7] it is clear that such support did emerge, was sustained (at least until late 1987 to early 1988), and was of great significance in moving the legislation forward. By the spring of 1987, the High Risk bills *appeared* to have the momentum and support which would lead to their passage; this view was certainly evident among supporters of the legislation. For example, in March 1987, "Senate and House staffs expect[ed] both bills to pass after various amendments [were] ironed out to appease some prominent opponents and to head off a veto by President Reagan" (*OSH Reporter* 1987a:1186-87). House Democratic Labor Whip Pat Williams stated "I can guarantee you that the House is going to pass this bill [H.R. 162]" (*OSH Reporter* 1987b:739). This optimism also extended to the Senate where a senior AFL-CIO spokesman maintained that "It's going to pass . . . the votes are there to pass this bill [S.79]" (Matlack 1987:832).

In October 1987, the House debated H.R. 162 at length. At that time, Republican opponents of the bill in the House led by Congressmen Jeffords (R-Vt.) and Henry (R-Mich.) proposed an "amendment in the nature of a substitute [bill]" (*Congressional Record* 1987:H8638). After a lengthy debate, the substitute bill was defeated by a vote of "ayes 191, noes 234, not voting 8" (*Congressional Record* 1987:H8657). The next day, the Democratic version of

H.R. 162 passed the House by a 225 to 186 vote. However, throughout the House proceedings, the business community's majority opposition to the legislation began to assert itself.

The Corporate Opposition Reacts To Business Support

As previously noted, when the High Risk Act was first introduced, the business community response was one of united and universal opposition. The importance of the High Risk issue to the corporate sector and the perceived need to ensure its defeat were reflected in the creation of a corporate opposition network known as the "Coalition on Occupational Disease Notification" (a network of over 200 trade associations and corporations that strongly opposed the legislation).[8] The coalition was organized in late 1985 and early 1986 in response to the introduction of and early hearings on H.R. 1309. According to sources within the organization, it was initially a contingency operation; its purpose was to coordinate and maximize business opposition to the legislation in case it developed any political momentum. NAM served as the organizational base for the coalition and NAM staff members provided support for and coordination of its activities.

Despite the early organization of the coalition network, it did not become actively and extensively involved in opposing the legislation until early 1987. According to a source within the organization, "[The legislation] was not perceived as something that was going to fly until about the beginning of 1987 and then people began to take it seriously because they did perceive that it could fly through [Congress]."

The emergence of significant business support for the High Risk bills in 1987 provided an edge of legitimacy and political support that made the legislation look like a real contender for congressional passage. However, it was the emergence of this same business support that also animated the coalition (along with the rest of the business community) and spurred it to higher and more effective levels of opposition. As the coordinator of the coalition stated, "their action initially 'undermined the effectiveness of the coalition,' but because of the attention it generated, it had the ironic effect of galvanizing business support for the coalition" (Victor 1988:1067).

With the majority of the business community opposing the High Risk legislation, the corporate and trade association splintering on the issue in early 1987 was viewed by most of the corporate community as an unacceptable threat to business cohesion and unity in a class-like sense. The interpretation of this development as the basis for increasingly vigorous corporate opposition to the legislation and the emergence of pressures to preserve corporate unity on the High Risk issue was shared by many informants. As a senior congressional source put it:

> The idea that Senators Metzenbaum and Kennedy could negotiate compromises and accommodations with some sectors of the business community was appallingly frightening to many corporations and their trade groups like the Business Roundtable, NAM, and the Chamber of Commerce. The reason the business community fought as hard as it did--way out of proportion to what the scope and implications of the legislation were--was because they did not ever want a precedent established in which a split in the business community led to the passage of a bill like this.

Once a consensus emerged within the corporate community that the High Risk bills contained not only significant and unacceptable redistributive features but also threatened to undermine the class-wide unity of business as well, an all-out mobilization of corporate resources to ensure the defeat of the legislation was mounted. The coalition was an active partner in these efforts. For example, to provide expert, politically effective testimony against H.R. 162, at the April 8, 1987, House hearings, the Coalition hired former Acting Assistant Secretary of Labor Pat Tyson. (Tyson had testified against H.R. 1309 on behalf of the Reagan administration in 1985.) In the Senate, the coalition orchestrated a "grass-roots" campaign which "flood[ed] Senate offices with letters, telegrams, phone calls, and personal visits. . . . nearly 10,000 . . . members from [one trade association] contacted senators urging them to support a filibuster" (Morehouse 1988b:842). At a more informal level, the coalition sponsored a briefing for Congressional staff members who wished to learn more about the reasons for business opposition to the legislation. The staffers heard from tort liability experts, an occupational epidemiologist, and also from Tyson as well as from the senior counsel to the American Mining Congress, Henry Chajet. All of the speakers emphasized the lack of need for the legislation as well as the great harm that it would inflict upon American businesses (*OSH Reporter* 1987a:1186-87).

The coalition engaged in other, less-publicized activities that were explicitly aimed at pressuring companies supporting the legislation to repudiate their policies and bring them back in line with the rest of the business community. As an example, informants reported that the coalition sent letters to various trade associations opposing the bills. These letters included lists of the associations' members with asterisks indicating which corporate members had split away from the trade associations' positions of opposition and were supporting the High Risk legislation. The reality of overlapping trade

association memberships among corporations meant that corporate executives
and trade association officials based in organizations that came out in support
of the legislation began to receive informal pressures from their peers in the
business community to switch their positions. This subtle but important
process produced results. A senior Senate staff member observed:

> The business community that opposed [the legislation] did a
> very good job of picking people off like within the CMA
> where some companies were also members of the American
> Petroleum Institute [API] which was adamantly opposed to
> the legislation. They picked off several of the big petroleum
> companies because of [pressure from other API members].

In addition to the coalition's efforts, individual corporate opponents of the
legislation engaged in "guerrilla-style" actions aimed at undermining support
for the legislation by opening up schisms within supportive trade associations.
For example, congressional sources reported that within the CMA, several
companies (primarily those CMA members which were also members of API)
either invoked a CMA organizational provision that allowed them to publicly
oppose the association's legislative policy position (the "Greenbriar clause") or
were openly sympathetic to companies that did invoke "Greenbriar." The
resulting divisions and conflicts helped to shift the association away from active
support for the legislation by early 1988 and, according to one source with
links to the organization, "nearly destroyed the CMA." Similar kinds of
internal divisions and conflicts were also reported by several sources to have
occurred within the American Electronics Association and the National Paint
and Coatings Association.

Corporate pressures for class-wide unity in opposition to the legislation
also took the form of implied threats against the jobs of corporate officials in
charge of those companies that supported the legislation. Sources close to this
aspect of the corporate campaign reported that statements were made by
corporate and political opponents of the legislation at functions, such as trade
association luncheons, suggesting that chief executive officers of companies
supporting the legislation should be fired. While informants could not (or
would not) confirm specific threats against specific individuals, even the
general suggestion of such possible severe sanctions is indicative of the
intensity of corporate insistence upon class-wide unity on the High Risk issue.

As the legislation moved to the Senate in early 1988, all informants who
commented on this aspect of the case agreed that the corporate mobilization
for class unity in opposition to the bill became increasingly effective. One
congressional source asserted that by the time the Senate began considering
the bill in March 1988, business support for the legislation had faded to the
point of being "an inch wide and an inch deep." Publicly, the positions of the

corporations and trade associations supporting the legislation were still on record, but little real effort was being put forward by business supporters on behalf of the bill. This situation illustrates the view of a Senate subcommittee staff member who observed that "the business community eventually jelled into an unbelievably cohesive, successful lobbying force."

High Risk Developments and Denouement: 1987-1988

Despite the emergence of ever more effective and vocal business opposition to the legislation, the High Risk bills continued to move ahead. As previously noted, H.R. 162 passed the House on October 15, 1987. In the Senate, S.79 also moved forward, but it faced mounting opposition aimed at slowing down its progress. For example, shortly after its introduction, Senator Quayle offered a substitute bill (S.382) which, while not taken seriously by either side, did help to provoke debate and slow the progress of S.79 (according to informants on both sides). In the subcommittee and in the full Senate Committee on Labor and Human Resources, Republican opponents of the legislation offered a number of amendments which were beaten back in each instance by the Democratic majority on the committee (U.S. Congress: Senate, 1987b:42-49). The revised form of S.79 supported by Senator Metzenbaum was approved by the Labor and Human Resources Committee by mid-1987 and the committee report was filed in September.

Even as the High Risk bills moved forward and the political struggles intensified in late 1987 and early 1988, opponents of the legislation were confident that it would never become law. If the corporate campaign against the legislation in the Congress failed, business groups were reasonably certain that their interests would be served by a presidential veto. This assurance derived from the knowledge that the White House opposed the legislation and was known to be receptive to the idea of a veto. In fact, the veto threat was repeated several times as the High Risk legislation was being considered. For example, at one point, just prior to House passage of H.R. 162, "six cabinet members and the head of the Small Business Administration signed a letter to Speaker Jim Wright (D-Tex) . . . saying they would recommend a veto" (Knudsen 1987:2513). In a reference to this action and others by Reagan administration officials, Congressman Jeffords (R-Vt.) stated, "This bill will be vetoed if it ever reaches the President's desk" (*Congressional Record* 1987:H8620).

Although a presidential veto was a likely prospect, congressional sources indicated that it was "a card that business would rather not play" (unless it became absolutely necessary as a last resort). This was the case because, as one source for a health association pointed out, it was conceivable to corporate opponents that if the legislation passed both the House and the Senate, the complex dynamics of politics and the public health image of the legislation *could* make a presidential veto uncertain. Therefore, following House passage of H.R. 162, the business opposition moved to ensure an outcome favorable to corporate interests in the Senate by pursuing a two-pronged strategy: (1) the utilization of political allies to mount a filibuster against the bill and (2) the cultivation of enough Senate votes to ensure the defeat of cloture votes to end the filibuster. The likelihood of corporate success in this effort was enhanced by business PAC contributions to Senate candidates which in the 1985-86 election cycle amounted to over $27 million compared to about $8 million in labor PAC contributions (FEC 1988:2).

Senator Orrin Hatch (R-Utah) led the filibuster. His publicly stated reasons for opposing S. 79 centered around its alleged duplication of existing federal efforts in occupational health and safety and the litigation-related damage it would inflict upon American firms (*Congressional Record* 1988c: S3226-3227). However, Senator Metzenbaum implied that Senator Hatch and other Senate opponents of S.79 were acting on the basis of very different motives:

> A vote against this bill is a vote for the high-paid and well-heeled lobbyists who are doing so much to try and defeat the legislation. If the Senator [Hatch] is with the workers . . . then I think he ought to reconsider and vote for this bill" (*Congressional Record* 1988b:S3179).

Ultimately, even Senator Hatch briefly departed from his publicly stated reasons for opposing S.79 and acknowledged the political realities involved with the legislation: "We all know why people are voting for and against this bill; it is because of political pressure as far as I can see" (*Congressional Record* 1988b:S3163). Although his motives for leading the filibuster cannot be known with certainty, Senator Hatch was reported by several informants to have a long-standing reputation within the Washington, D.C., policy-making community as a friend of corporate interests and as an opponent of most legislation favored by organized labor. Thus, it is not surprising that corporate opponents of the High Risk Act were able to enlist him as the point man in defense of business interests by leading the filibuster against S.79.[9]

Informants both in and out of Congress reported that to ensure the success of the filibuster, the corporate campaign focused upon several southern Democratic Senators whose positions were likely to be crucial in cloture votes. A major success in this effort was the apparent defection of Senator Dale Bumpers (D-Mo.) to the opposition camp. Several congressional sources asserted that Senator Bumpers had initially indicated a commitment to support

S.79. During the Senate deliberations, however, Senator Bumpers began to privately urge that Senate Democrats oppose the legislation, and he later took credit for helping to defeat the bill by upholding the filibuster: "I honestly think that I tilted 14 Democratic votes against the bill, which was its death knell" (Cohen 1989:175).[10] In the end the filibuster, with the support of key southern Democratic senators, led to the bill's ultimate "defeat by debate." After losing four cloture votes (the last one on March 29, 1988, by a forty two "yea" to fifty two "nay" margin), Senator Metzenbaum withdrew the bill from consideration.[11]

It is difficult to prove the existence and nature of direct linkages between corporate opponents of S.79 and individual senators who voted against cloture on the bill. However, the results clearly indicate that at least on this issue, the business community was able to mobilize its resources and win the political support it needed to obtain the outcome it favored in the Senate. The success of the corporate sector on the High Risk issue is in keeping with a tradition of business victories in conflicts over legislation that includes actual or potential redistributive features perceived by the business community as harmful to its interests (Vogel 1983; Szasz 1986).

The use of the veto threat to undercut support for the High Risk bills and the extent of political support for the filibuster in the Senate illustrates the ability of the corporate community to build upon and mobilize institutional arrangements favoring its interests to obtain policy decisions which it desires. At the same time the outcome also underscores a key structural handicap confronting labor in policy conflicts, viz, its minority position within the policy-making community; unions represent only 2 percent of organized lobby groups while corporations and trade associations comprise 72 percent of the Washington, D.C., lobby community (Schlozman and Tierney 1986:77). The array of institutional biases favoring business means that when the stakes on a policy issue are high, labor, in the absence of unusual historical circumstances (e.g., large percentages of unionized workers and/or political-economic crises), often lacks the resources, even with middle-class coalitional allies, to resist determined corporate campaigns against legislation that would support the interests of workers.

5

THE FOCAL ACTORS: DESCRIPTIONS, LINKAGES, AND ANALYSIS

I submit that if a million people in the so-called middle or professional classes were dying each decade of preventable occupational disease, and if nearly four million were being disabled, there would long ago have been such a hue and cry for remedial action that if the Congress had not heeded it, vast numbers of its members would have been turned out of office.

Testimony of Paul Brodeur, author of *Expendable Americans*. OSHA Congressional Oversight Hearing. U.S. Congress: House, 1974, p. 241.

INTRODUCTION

Nearly twenty years ago in *Death on the Job*, Daniel Berman characterized the occupational health and safety professions as "the captive specialties" (Berman 1978: 94). His point was that most professionals in these areas were hostages; they owed their jobs and incomes to corporations which had little real interest in protecting the health and safety of workers. On the basis of research paralleling that of Berman, Paul Brodeur concluded that among corporations the prevailing view was that workers were "Expendable Americans" (Brodeur, 1974). Brodeur also testified at a congressional hearing that many elements of the health and safety professions complicitly shared such a view and were partners in "a pervasive effort . . . to suppress and ignore medical information concerning hazardous substances that are . . . killing . . . [and] disabling [hundreds of thousands of American workers each year]" (U.S. Congress: House, 1974:236).

Those accusations addressed conditions as they appeared to those authors then--nearly two decades ago. What about now? What do the data reveal about the characteristics, interorganizational linkages, and policy decisions of key professional groups concerned with occupational health and safety today? The information reported in this chapter initiates the process of assessing the autonomous versus captive status of health and safety professional associations in the contemporary period.

We begin with a descriptive overview of selected structural characteristics of the focal actors which highlights various similarities and differences among these organizations. Next we turn to a consideration of variations in the internal policy-making procedures of the associations. Finally, two tables are presented which summarize the structural linkage subtypes associated with each organization and provide the bases for a discussion and assessment of the two key research hypotheses outlined in chapter 2.

SELECTED CHARACTERISTICS
OF THE FOCAL ACTORS

Each of the seven associations is a tax-exempt, nonprofit corporation with a membership composed primarily of individuals. The organizations are typically incorporated within and bound by the laws of the states where the headquarters are located. State laws generally require these organizations to "observe various organizational and operational requirements . . . [such as] annual meetings must be held, minutes must be kept, and annual reports must be filed by incorporated organizations in most states" (Jacobs 1986:18).

Table 5.1 presents an alphabetically ordered overview of the seven associations in terms of selected characteristics related to their membership totals, income levels and sources, and Internal Revenue Service (IRS) tax-exempt designations.

Discussion: Table 5.1

As table 5.1 indicates, the membership size of the seven organizations ranges from 3,200 (ACGIH) to over 250,000 (AMA). The criteria for membership varies from an expressed interest in health issues and a willingness to pay membership dues (e.g., APHA), to more stringent requirements such as the possession of a professional degree (and license--e.g., AAOHN, AMA, AOMA) and/or employment within a specialized occupation (e.g., AIHA, ACGIH, ASSE).

In addition to highlighting large variations in membership size, the table also points out the wide range in association incomes. One of the most strik-

Table 5.1
Selected Characteristics of the Focal Actors

Association	Membership size: 1987	Total Annual Income: 1987 dollars[a]	Membership Dues: % of income	Conference, Workshop, Accreditation fees, Publ. Sales, & Advertising: % of income	Internal Revenue Code Tax-exempt Designation[b]
1. AAOHN	11,000	1,442,334	70%	29%	501(c)(6)
2. ACGIH	3,200	505,951	21%	67%	501(c)(6)
3. AIHA	7,000	3,317,753	8%	85%	501(c)(6)
4. AMA	256,000	135,391,753	46%	39%	501(c)(6)
5. AOMA[c]	4,300	1,243,299	35%	61%	501(c)(6)
6. APHA	55,000	5,474,493[d]	27%	43%	501(c)(3)
7. ASSE	18,800	2,714,735	40%	50%	501(c)(6)

[a] The income figures are derived from information reported in the organizations' IRS form 990 tax returns.
[b] An IRS 501(c)(6) designation denotes the organization as a "business league" designed to "promote common business interest[s]." (U.S. Dept. of Treasury 1989:7751-107) The 501(c)(3) designation applies to non-profit organizations "operated exclusively for religious, charitable, scientific testing for public safety, literary or educational purposes." (Ibid:7751-27).
[c] The AOMA merged in 1988 with the American Academy of Occupational Medicine to form the American College of Occupational Medicine; the membership total for the ACOM is reported to be 4,700.
[d] This figure is for 1986; the 1987 figure was unavailable.

ing features of the table is the vast difference between the financial resources of the AMA compared with those of the other six organizations. As an illustration of these extreme differences, it is interesting to note that in 1987, the total annual income of the ACGIH ($505,951) was less than the annual salary of the AMA's top staff member, Dr. James H. Sammons. As Executive Vice President of the AMA, he was paid $697,718. The extent of the gap between the AMA's resources and that of the other associations is clearly apparent from the sums reported in the Total Annual Income column. Looking more closely at information reported in the AMA IRS Form 990 tax return (but not reported in the table), we find that the category of relatively minor, "Other Revenue" for the AMA (e.g., royalties, employee cafeteria sales, and so forth) totaled $11,435,894 in 1987. While this amount was a very small fraction of total AMA income for 1987, it was nearly equal to the total income for all of the other six associations added together ($14,698,555).[1]

Another important variation in association characteristics pointed out by table 5.1 involves the sources of association income. For example, the AAOHN received the 70 percent of its 1987 revenues from individual membership dues. At the same time, the AIHA received only 8 percent of its income from membership dues with 85 percent of the total derived from various organizational activities and other sources. As the fifth column in the table indicates, four of the seven associations' annual revenues are derived mainly from income sources related to organizationally sponsored activities such conferences, workshops, and publication sales (ACGIH, AIHA, AOMA, ASSE).[2]

A final variation in association characteristics addressed by table 5.1 involves the organizations' IRS tax-exempt status. These designations are reminders that professional societies operate within a legal environment that includes not only state laws but also various federal regulations and guidelines that relate to both income tax reporting requirements and lobbying and political activities.[3]

The Internal Revenue Code (IRC) classification of tax-exempt, nonprofit organizations includes several subtypes. As the table indicates, six of the seven associations have received IRC classifications as 501(c)(6) organizations. This designation applies to "business leagues" which the IRC defines as "an association of persons . . . having a common business interest, whose purpose it is to promote the common business interest" (U.S. Department of the Treasury 1989:7751-107). By contrast, the 501(c)(3) designation applies to nonprofit organizations that are "organized and operated exclusively for religious, charitable, scientific testing for public safety, literary, or educational purposes" (Ibid:7751-27). The IRC designation is directly related to federal restrictions applicable to organizational lobbying activities concerning legislation such as the High Risk bills. In general, the 501(c)(6) designation involves few restrictions on organizational lobbying and political activities. However, the

501(c)(3) classification involves more detailed income reporting requirements and explicit expenditure limitations concerning organizational lobbying and political activities. (See Webster 1983, 1985, and Jacobs 1986:455 for more detailed discussions of these distinctions and related restrictions.)

To illustrate this point on reporting requirements, it is interesting to note that all six of the 501(c)(6) associations responded "no" to item #83 on IRS Form 990: "Did the organization spend any amounts in attempts to influence public opinion about legislative matters or referendums?" (IRS 990, Part VII "Other Information"). By contrast the APHA, which as a 501(c)(3) organization uses a slightly different 990 Form, answered "yes" to item #1, Part III: "During the year, have you attempted to influence national, state, or local legislation, including any attempt to influence public opinion on a legislative matter of referendum?" (IRS Form 990, Schedule A, Part III, "Statement About Activities"). In a statement attached to the 990 tax return regarding its "yes" answer, the APHA stated "The [legislative] . . . activities constitute an insignificant portion of the overall activities of the American Public Health Association. Expenses incurred were nominal and were not segregated and readily available from the Association's records" (1986 APHA Form 990 tax return, Schedule A Statement, 21/31/86).

These data underscore the reality that none of the associations are particularly eager to call attention to their policy involvement activities or volunteer any more information than absolutely necessary concerning the details of any resources which they may have committed in attempts to influence the legislative process. Even the APHA's open admission on its tax return of participating in the development of legislative issues was qualified by its characterization of these actions as representing only a very limited feature of its overall activities. Despite this public stance, as we will see, all seven of the associations were involved to a greater or lesser extent with developing the High Risk legislation (and, in some cases, other legislative issues as well). However, the status of the six associations incorporated as 501(c)(6) tax-exempt organizations placed few legal limits on their legislative and/or political activities. It is clear that their interpretations of IRS reporting rules did not require them to attach statements concerning the nature and extent of their involvement with the High Risk legislative issue (or any others) or report any expenses which may have been incurred as a result of such activities.

ASSOCIATION POLICY-MAKING PROCESSES

Based upon interviews with representatives from the seven associations and various documentary sources, it is clear that the leadership and staff in these organizations have continuing interests in and concerns with a variety of political and policy issues. These interests and concerns embrace both state and federal policies or programs related to their members' areas of expertise and their organizations. While some associations may be proactive on some issues (i.e., initiate legislation), association policies related to public issues and legislation typically follow a pattern that begins with a policy-tracking and/or monitoring process.

The policy-tracking process is highly variable among the seven focal actors. As might be expected, those with the most resources are best organized for this purpose. For example, the AMA maintains state and federal policy-development divisions at its headquarters (in Illinois) and also a lobbying unit in Washington, D.C. The APHA monitors policy through its Washington, D.C., staff and through its numerous interest sections and through other informal contacts. Two organizations (AIHA and ASSE) retain the services of an attorney, David A. Swankin, who tracks Washington, D.C., developments of interest to health and safety professionals and writes a monthly column for the AIHA and ASSE journals (e.g., Swankin 1988: A-8, 1989:5). The AAOHN, in 1987, "contracted with the Washington, D.C.-based public affairs agency Manning Selage & Lee to work on a combined governmental affairs and public relations program" (*AAOHN Journal* 1987a:130).[4]

The process of monitoring relevant legislative and/or administrative proposals at the state or federal levels is typically linked to the associations' internal policy-making processes whenever it attracts the attention of an association's leadership on a particular issue or bill. At that point, the formal procedures (which exist for all seven associations) for considering and adopting policies on legislative issues may be set in motion. The details of association policy establishment vary, but most begin with a leadership referral of an issue to a committee, which is then followed by a report back to the leadership. The process typically concludes with a ratification or rejection vote by either the organization's officers or board of directors and/or the organizational membership in attendance at an annual conference.[5] However, despite the existence of these "ideal-type" procedures, they are not always followed on every issue for various reasons.

One complicating factor in the policy-making process is legal in nature. This means that while formal association policy-making procedures, as outlined in the organizations' bylaws, are typically democratic (in the sense of providing members with a role), most states require that associations designate an organizational entity that is accountable for association policy-decisions (Jacobs 1986:17, 80). In practical terms this means that the board of directors and/or trustees is the final legal authority for most policy matters. Also, at the informal level, (for a variety of reasons including the reality that the association leadership tends to be more elite than the membership) board members' preferences tend to be major factors in determining association policies on most issues under most circumstances. As one association executive stated "The formal process is usually too cumbersome on most issues; the board is really where policy is made in most associations."

A second factor complicating the policy-making process is contextual in nature. Sometimes events move faster than routine policy procedures can accommodate. For example, the AIHA involvement with the initial High Risk bill occurred as a result of a request from the House Subcommittee on Health and Safety for testimony from the association with only eleven days advance notice. Under these (or similar) circumstances, an association's leadership and/or staff may make policy choices with little or no input from the membership. Policies adopted in such situations may or may not be subject to later endorsement through the usual policy process. (As we will see, this appeared to be the case with the High Risk legislation for at least two organizations--the AIHA and AMA.)

In interviews, association staff members emphasized that regardless of the details of the formal policy-making process, the association leadership (and the senior staff) are the central actors in establishing association policies. This situation obtains for several reasons related primarily to their position of authority over organizational resources including access to and control over the flow of information through, for example, the organization's publications and communications. Thus, while the membership may be called upon to ratify policy positions adopted by an organization's leadership, association staff members tended to view such votes as mere formalities which "officially" legitimate the preferences of the officers and board members.[6]

Among the focal actors, the policy-setting leadership typically consisted of governing boards composed of the elected officers and a group of directors and/or trustees. Membership in these policy-setting entities ranged in size from eight (ACGIH) to twenty five (ASSE), with an average of approximately eighteen. One exception of note was the APHA governing council which included approximately 190 members. However, for this organization, the much smaller "executive board" of nineteen elected officers and directors was used in making comparisons with the other associations.

Based upon information from association representatives and various other sources,[7] it was clear that the leadership of the seven organizations (i.e., the officers and directors or trustees--sometimes in conjunction with the senior staff) was *the* dominant force in shaping association policy and resource-commitment decisions concerning the High Risk legislation. In some cases the leadership initiated policy directions on the legislation from the beginning, and in other cases became more involved in the latter stages of the development of the bills. However, there were no cases with evidence to indicate that any association's policy decisions on the High Risk legislation were *membership driven* (i.e., the result of an active membership pressing a passive leadership into action).

ASSESSMENT OF THE RESEARCH HYPOTHESES

Tables 5.2 and 5.3 provide summaries of information related to the structural linkage factor subtypes and the associations' basic policy decisions (table 5.2) and resource-commitment levels (table 5.3) concerning the High Risk legislation. The tables also include Pattern Congruence columns where Consistent, Semiconsistent, or Inconsistent designations are used as a means of providing general, global assessments of the extent to which there is a "fit" between the predictions of the research hypotheses and the observed outcomes. That is, these terms summarize how closely the relationships between the "positive" and "negative" structural linkage patterns and the focal actors' basic policy and resource-commitment decisions correspond to the hypothesized predictions.

As table 5.2 indicates, among those associations adopting Basic Policy Positions of Support for the legislation (the first four listed), Consistent or Semiconsistent Pattern Congruence designations appear for three of the four cases (AAOHN, ACGIH, APHA). For the AMA, the structural linkage pattern is indicative of an *expected* Neutral/Opposed policy position.[8] However, the AMA position of Support makes it an Inconsistent case (i.e., with our posited expectations). (The possible reasons for this apparent inconsistency are considered in chapter six.)

Table 5.2 also indicates that among associations adopting Neutral/Opposed policy positions, (the last three listed--AIHA, AOMA,[9] ASSE) a Consistent Pattern Congruence designation appears for all three cases. It is clear that for these cases the structural linkage patterns are virtually mirror images of those associated with three of the first four cases (except for the AMA) that supported the legislation. This comparison *across* case categories combined with the results observed *within* case categories provides strong support for our first hypothesis. Both types of comparisons lend support to the conclusion that structural linkage combinations involving predominantly positive or negative subtypes are influential in shaping associations' basic policy decisions in positive or negative directions.

In short, except for the AMA, the results reported in table 5.2 are generally consistent with and supportive of our first hypothesis concerning the posited effects of the structural linkages. This is especially true insofar as combinations of linkage factor subtypes are indicative of relative freedom from or dependence upon the corporate sector for association membership employment, leadership personnel, and organizational resources.

Table 5.2
Structural Linkages & Basic Policy Decisions

Association	Structural Linkage Factor Summary			Basic Policy Positions	Pattern Congruence
	Sponsorship	Interpenetration	Resource Dependency		
1. AAOHN	Corporate (-) (86%)	Low (+) (25%)	Internal-Dependent (+)	Support (+)	Semi-consistent
2. ACGIH	Nonprofit (+) (100%)	Low (+) (0%)	External-Nonprofit (+)	Support (+)	Consistent
3. AMA	Corporate (-) (87%)	Low (+) (0%)	External-Corporate (-)	Support (+)	Inconsistent
4. APHA	Nonprofit (+) (80%)	Low (+) (0%)	External-Nonprofit (+)	Support (+)	Consistent
5. AIHA	Corporate (-) (75%)	High (-) (94%)	External-Corporate (-)	Neutral/Opposed (-)	Consistent
6. AOMA	Corporate (-) (80%)	High (-) (95%)	External-Corporate (-)	Neutral/Opposed (-)	Consistent
7. ASSE	Corporate (-) (80%)	High (-) (80%)[a]	External-Corporate (-)	Neutral/Opposed (-)	Consistent

[a] This figure includes officers/directors who own and/or manage private consulting firms.

Table 5.3

Structural Linkages & Resource-Commitment Levels

Array Rank	Association	Structural Linkage[a] Factors			Basic Policy Position	Resource[b] Commitment	Pattern Congruence
		S	I	RD			
1.	AAOHN	S -	I +	RD +	Support +	Strong + + +	Semi-consistent
2.	APHA	S +	I +	RD +	Support +	Strong + + +	Consistent
3.	AMA	S -	I +	RD -	Support +	Nominal +	Inconsistent
4.	ACGIH	S +	I +	RD +	Support +	Nominal +	Semi-consistent
5.	ASSE	S -	I -	RD -	Neutral/ Opposed -	Neutral =	Semi-consistent
6.	AOMA	S -	I -	RD -	Neutral/ Opposed -	Nominal -	Semi-consistent
7.	AIHA	S -	I -	RD -	Neutral/ Opposed -	Strong - - -	Consistent

[a] Structural Linkage Factors: S = Sponsorship; I = Interpenetration; RD = Resource Dependency.

[b] Resource-Commitment Levels vary as follows: support levels are designated as: Strong + + +; Moderate + +; Nominal +; No Evidence of Resources Committed: Neutral =; Opposition Levels are designated as: Strong - - -; Moderate - -; Nominal -.

Table 5.3 ranks all seven focal actors according to the extent of association resources committed on behalf of each organization's basic policy position on the High Risk bills throughout the 1985-88 period. The listing begins with the association which the interview and archival evidence indicates was most strongly supportive of the legislation (AAOHN) and ends with the one most strongly opposed to the legislation (AIHA). The results reported in table 5.3. indicate that the levels of resources committed by six of the seven cases on behalf of their basic policy decisions are generally consistent with and supportive of the expectations of our second research hypothesis--with some qualifications.

Looking at the Pattern Congruence column, we can see that for the two Consistent cases (APHA, AIHA), the relationships between the extent of the resource-commitment levels (for the respective policies of Support and Opposition) and the observed structural linkage patterns were virtually invariant and closely in line with the expectations of our second hypothesis. Given the observed structural linkage subtypes associated with the four Semiconsistent cases (AAOHN, ACGIH, ASSE, AOMA), the resource-com-mitment levels *trended* in the directions predicted by our second hypothesis. However, since the resource-commitment levels were highly variable for these cases, totally invariant patterns were not present and the Semiconsistent designation was applied. The AMA's Inconsistent designation indicates that on the basis of its structural linkage pattern, the resource-commitment level trended in a direction that was the reverse of what we expected; thus, once again the AMA represents a "problem" case in terms of predicted outcomes.

Taken together, the results reported in tables 5.2 and 5.3 indicate that, for the most part, the relationships between the structural linkage patterns and association policy decisions are largely consistent with and supportive of our hypotheses and the general expectations of our theory. Although the basic outlines of patterns and trends involving the relationship between the structural linkages and policy outcomes are clear, the semiconsistent and inconsistent cases indicate some instances where invariant patterns do not occur.

CONCLUSIONS

Despite wide variations on a number of characteristics, when examined in terms of the patterns of structural linkages to the public or private sectors, the seven associations demonstrate some remarkable consistencies concerning the nature and extent of their basic policy and resource-commitment decisions towards the High Risk legislation. With some exceptions, tables 5.2 and 5.3 make it apparent that the posited effects of the structural linkages upon both the associations' basic policy decisions and resource-commitment levels are largely supported by the data. This suggests that the model developed in chapter 2 has a high degree of explanatory power. However, it is also clear from the data that there are gaps and inconsistencies between what was expected and what was observed in terms of the effects of these linkages. It is our view that the inconsistencies in the results are reflective not so much of serious flaws in our theory as they are of problems with measuring association policy and resource-commitment decisions and the complexity of the policy process.

The reality of the policy-formation process as a dynamic, multilevel process complicates efforts to ascertain with precision exact levels of legislative support or opposition among organizations--including professional societies. The procedures by which policies are formulated makes the content of any given piece of legislation (including the High Risk bills) a kind of moving target (Neustadtl 1990). That is, as the authors and supporters of a bill seek political allies, trade-offs and compromises are made which in turn affect the composition of the cast of supporters and opponents. At the same time, organizational opposition to or support for legislation exists at different levels and may take many different forms.

Taken together, these complexities make it difficult to pin down and measure, in an unambiguous fashion, the policy positions and resource-commitment levels adopted by the focal actors on the High Risk legislation. (The same holds true for other organizations on other bills as well.) When we also consider the wide variations in structural characteristics among the seven associations, it becomes clear how difficult it is to prove definitively that the structural linkages alone produced consistently predictable effects upon their policy and resource-commitment decisions. Even so, the consistency of the data tying the structural linkage patterns and decision outcomes in the face of such complexities and structural variations indicates that our model is both compelling and parsimonious. It provides a useful and relatively simple handle for reducing a bewildering array of *potential* influences upon association policy decisions to a small number of what the data suggest are centrally important, causal factors. Of course, the structural linkages are not the complete story-- as we will see in the next two chapters--but they do provide a manageable core of concepts for identifying and tracing important causal linkages where professional association policy decisions on controversial, redistributive occupational health legislation are concerned.

The next two chapters provide contextualized case narratives of the policy involvement activities and decisions of the seven associations. These accounts clarify and illustrate the evidence used as the bases for determining the policy and resource-commitment designations applied to the focal actors and utilized in tables 5.2 and 5.3. At the same time, the narratives also inquire into the reasons for the observed departures from expected invariant patterns as reported in tables 5.2 and 5.3. They consider the role of contextual factors in shaping departures from hypothesized outcomes in order to determine if, or to what extent, our theoretical model is in need of modifications.

6

CASE NARRATIVES:
FOUR WHO PLAYED

From a governmental perspective, we ought to be ashamed of ourselves, because in the foreign jurisdictions, Sweden, Germany, France, and Italy, workers have a right to be notified of these [occupational] hazards and are notified of these hazards.

> Testimony of Dr. Nicholas A. Ashford, APHA representative, H.R. 1309 Hearings. U.S. Congress: House, 1985, p. 274.

INTRODUCTION

This chapter presents detailed accounts of evidence and information related to the policy and resource-commitment decisions of the four associations which supported the High Risk legislation. Each narrative sketch is divided into three sections. First, a review of evidence derived from association sources is outlined to illustrate and support the summary policy and resource-commitment designations utilized in tables 5.2 and 5.3 in chapter 5 for the four supportive associations. The second section ("Another View") consists of impressions derived from other policy-making participants concerning their views on the involvement of each supportive association with the High Risk legislation. The third section ("Interpretation") presents an interpretative overview which considers the conjunctural influence of the structural linkages, contextual factors, and ethical codes and principles upon each association's policy and resource-commitment decisions.

AMERICAN ASSOCIATION OF
OCCUPATIONAL HEALTH NURSES

The AAOHN's involvement with the High Risk legislation dates back to the 1985 bill. Prior to the introduction of H.R. 1309, the AAOHN was actively trying to get OSHA's Hazard Communication Standard (issued in November 1983) revised to include occupational health nurses in that document's definition of a "health professional."[1] As a result of the involvement by the association on that issue, the staff and leadership developed and cultivated a number of political contacts in Washington, D.C.; they also began to monitor more closely federal policy developments that might be relevant to the interests of the organization's leadership and members.

In an interview, an AAOHN staff member reported that the staff and leadership learned of the High Risk bill in early 1985 via a report in the *OSH Reporter*. To their dismay they learned that occupational health nurses were not among the health professionals to be included on the Risk Assessment Board which the bill would create. This circumstance was similar to the Hazard Communication Standard issue and was a cause of great concern in the organization. As a result of that situation, the AAOHN's senior staff contacted Congressman Gaydos and his staff associated with the House Health and Safety Subcommittee. The result was a negotiated *quid pro quo* arrangement whereby Congressman Gaydos agreed to amend the bill to include an occupational health nurse on the Risk Assessment Board in exchange for the political support of the AAOHN. The AAOHN's board of directors approved of this agreement prior to the 1985 hearings on the bill. The stage was then set for the following exchange during the 1985 hearings between Congressman Gaydos and the AAOHN Executive Director, Matilda Babbitz. Mr. Gaydos (speaking): "May I make you one promise? You help us with our problems on the floor, and I will help you with your problem." Ms. Babbitz (speaking): "That is a deal. That is perfectly OK. I am delighted to have this opportunity" (U.S. Congress: House, 1985:345).

Following the 1985 hearings, the AAOHN remained an active supporter of the High Risk legislation. Throughout 1986, the organization continued to track the progress of the legislation as the House bill was being revised and the Senate version was being prepared. In January 1987, the AAOHN board of directors "voted unanimously... to support 'actively' efforts to pass a high risk occupational disease bill in the 100th Congress" (*AAOHN News* 1987a:1). In the 1987 House and Senate hearings on H.R. 162 and S.79, Ms. Babbitz, representing the AAOHN, testified again in favor of the High Risk bills. Also, "in other action, AAOHN... sent letters to 46 Senators and 87 House members urging cosponsorship of the bills" (*AAOHN News* 1987a:1).

In addition to congressional testimony supporting the High Risk legislation, the organization's leadership also initiated an extensive grassroots letter writing campaign on behalf of the House and Senate bills in 1987. In a September 24, 1987, letter to Congressman Gaydos, the executive director of AAOHN stated:

> The Board of Directors of AAOHN, meeting September 16, 1987, in Atlanta, reaffirmed our position in support of H.R. 162. In addition, the board approved the following action by the association: [1] Sending letters to members of the U.S. House urging them to vote for H.R.162. [2] Requesting the presidents of our more than 170 local, state, and regional constituent associations across the country to send letters to appropriate members of the House urging a positive vote on H.R. 162. (U.S. Congress: House, 1985-88).

The AAOHN staff also played a role in an informal coalition of labor unions, environmental groups, and other health associations (such as the American Lung Association and the American Cancer Society) in urging passage of the legislation. However, given the AAOHN's limited resources and its headquarters location (Atlanta, Georgia), the organization could not maintain a continuous presence on Capitol Hill. Even so, interview and documentary evidence indicates that it did allocate a significant amount of staff time and organizational resources in support of the legislation up to the very end. In late 1987, after H.R. 162 had passed the House and as the Senate was preparing to consider S.79, "AAOHN President Elisabeth M. Bodnar [sent] letter[s] to all 100 members of the U.S. Senate . . . support[ing] S.79. [The] . . . AAOHN [also] . . . asked presidents of constituent organizations to write letters to their Senators urging support for the legislation" (*AAOHN News* 1987b:1). This activist stance in support of the legislation continued until the filibuster ended the bill's prospects for passage in the Senate.

AAOHN: Another View

The AAOHN's active role in supporting the High Risk legislation was confirmed by representatives from a variety of organizations which also participated in the High Risk case. For example, senior staff members affiliated with the congressional subcommittees and within organized labor characterized the AAOHN as "very active and supportive of the legislation." These sources recounted not only the AAOHN's testimony and letter writing campaigns but also commented on the association's utilization of political connections with key members of Congress to help improve the legislation's prospects for passage. In one instance a congressional source pointed out that in the Senate "the occupational health nurses have a very good relationship with Senator Inouye [(D-HI)]. Senator Inouye was helpful at a couple of key points. . . . [They also] have individual relationships with others that turned out to be useful."

AAOHN: Interpretation

The evidence indicates that structural linkages, political considerations, and contextual factors were all relevant and important to the AAOHN's active involvement with the High Risk legislation. For example, although the associations' membership is based largely in the private sector (80 percent), the relative absence of private sector interpenetration (25 percent), and the absence of extensive financial dependence upon the same sector are important features which together provide the structural basis for *relative* autonomy vis-à-vis external corporate interests.[2] On controversial issues such as the High Risk legislation, the association leadership was better positioned to determine policy on bases other than resource dependency obligations to corporate patrons.

For the AAOHN the structural linkage ties reflected a pattern indicative of an important measure of organizational autonomy, but not necessarily of interests insofar as policy decisions on the High Risk legislation was concerned. Information from organizational documents and informants indicated that the commitment of the AAOHN's leadership to the High Risk legislation was also part of a broader "professionalization project" aimed at enhancing the image and prestige of occupational health nurses.[3] Commenting on the position of occupational health nurses in the past and in the future, the AAOHN president wrote:

> Throughout the early years, occupational health nursing was
> a silent, invisible profession. Our opinions were not sought
> . . . [there was] a lack of recognition and utilization of the
> occupational health nurse as a manager. In the next decade,
> occupational health nurses will receive greater recognition as
> health care managers (Bodnar 1988:21).

The interest of the AAOHN in increasing the professional image and stature of occupational health nurses preceded the High Risk legislation and was apparent in interviews with sources both in and out of the organization. For example, a senior staff member with another association commented on the AAOHN's support for the High Risk bills: "They have become very proactive and so they're trying to get their message across that they're somebody to deal with. They feel like second-class citizens so what they've done is to support this [legislation]."

The AAOHN's project of advancing the professional status of occupational health nurses included active involvement in a variety of political endeavors. The organization's primary aim was to incorporate AAOHN members within a variety of federal agencies concerned with occupational health issues. The specific objectives of this strategy included increasing the numbers and visibility of occupational health nurses within federal agencies--especially at policy-making levels. This would serve as a means of further legitimizing and enhancing the professional status, recognition, and acceptance of nurses as full partners within the community of occupational health professionals. Insofar as the High Risk legislation was concerned, the organization's leadership was clearly interested in the potential distributive-type benefits that could result from the inclusion of an occupational health nurse on the Risk Assessment Board. This position, along with previous AAOHN gains in recognition and representation within OSHA-related agencies, would add another step in the direction of further enhancing the prestige, opportunities, and, very likely, the income levels of its members.[4] Another incentive for supporting the legislation involved provisions added in later versions of the bills that would "allow the federal government to make grants or enter into contractual agreements with schools of nursing to upgrade academic programs in occupational health nursing" (*AAOHN News* 1987b:1).

The evidence indicates that a confluence of structural conditions favoring organizational autonomy, political motivations and alliances, and propitious events and circumstances all contributed to the AAOHN's strong support for the High Risk legislation. Of these factors, the invisible reality of structural autonomy was never mentioned in the interviews as a factor related to the organization's ability to remain independent from corporate influence. However, it was alluded to by an informant within the AAOHN who pointed out that corporate pressures had been brought to bear on the association in an effort to convince the leadership to change the organization's policy on the legislation.[5] The ability of the AAOHN's leadership to resist such corporate pressures was at least partly due to the organization's relative independence from extensive structural linkages with the business community. Also, after the split within corporate ranks on the legislation in 1987, the AAOHN was not confronted with total unity in the business community on the issue. Since at least three AAOHN officers and board members worked for corporations that switched to positions of support for the legislation in 1987,[6] the leadership was not totally linked to corporations hostile to the legislation. This situation helped to reduce the isolation of the board on the High Risk issue and, thus, the intensity of corporate pressure on the leadership to modify the association's policies on the High Risk bills.

Insofar as the importance of ethical considerations upon AAOHN's support for the High Risk legislation is concerned, we find little evidence to indicate that ethics played a significant role in influencing association policy on this issue.[7] Ethical concerns were briefly cited in the AAOHN's congressional testimony as a basis for supporting the High Risk legislation: "the worker is the basic client from an ethical point of view" (U.S. Congress: House, 1985:344). However, ethics were virtually never mentioned during interviews as major factors motivating the association's support for the bills. Instead, the organization's political agenda including the professionalization project and the economic interests of the leadership and membership were repeatedly cited by informants as paramount concerns in this instance.

As a closing comment on this organization, it is interesting to consider the ironic consequences that would follow if the AAOHN should succeed in its quest for greater professional recognition and integration into corporate structures at higher management levels. A likely result of such success for the organization would be the loss of those structural features that undergirded its relative autonomy in this case and, thus, enabled it to actively support the High Risk bills.

AMERICAN PUBLIC HEALTH ASSOCIATION

The APHA's involvement with the High Risk legislation preceded the introduction of H.R. 1309. While the bill was being prepared, the staff of the House Subcommittee on Health and Safety contacted the APHA and requested their input. A subcommittee staff member noted that "We sought them out and the APHA has been very supportive. They helped tremendously in refining the whole [technical] approach to risk notification." At the subcommittee hearings on November 13, 1985, Dr. Nicholas A. Ashford testified on behalf of the APHA and expressed the organization's strong support for H.R. 1309. He also offered specific suggestions on how the bill could be modified and strengthened (U.S. Congress: House, 1985:266-275).

The APHA's participation in the development and support of the legislation was consistent with a long-standing policy by the APHA of supporting disease prevention in the workplace and more specifically with "the principle of workers' right-to-know of health risks associated with workplace hazardous exposures as expressed in a 1984 APHA position paper" (*The Nation's Health* 1986:8). On October 1, 1986, the APHA governing council adopted a specific policy statement (8607) which stated, in part, that the APHA "Endorses and supports enactment of the bills before the Congress to establish a federal program to accomplish worker notification objectives and provide appropriate support services" (*American Journal of Public Health* 1987:103-104).[8]

The APHA continued to support the High Risk legislation in 1987 and 1988 in both the House and Senate. On April 2, 1987, the organization sent letters signed by APHA President Ruth Roemer, J.D., to all members of the House and Senate expressing the association's strong support for the legislation. In part, the letters stated "In 1985, APHA testified in support of this legislation . . . We urge you to support the High Risk Occupational Disease Notification and Prevention Act of 1987 and look forward to working with you towards its passage" (U.S. Congress: Senate 1986-88).

The APHA newsletter monitored events related to the progress of the legislation in Congress and featured prominent reports on the topic (*The Nation's Health* 1987:1; 1988a; 1988b). While the bills were being considered in Congress, sources in the Washington, D.C., policy-making community reported that the APHA also provided lobbying support in the form of staff participation in joint strategy meetings with staff members from the AFL-CIO and other supportive organizations. Also, APHA staff visited the offices of individual Representatives and Senators urging their support for the legislation.

APHA: Another View

Several informants confirmed the activist stance of the APHA in support of the High Risk bills. Within the congressional subcommittees, Democratic staff members praised the organization's leadership not only for their support but also for assisting in refining the bill's technical and scientific sections. In their view, these efforts strengthened the bill and also helped to make it more acceptable to some members of the business community. Despite the fact that the organization did not testify in the 1987 hearings, a Democratic staff member supervising the progress of the bills stated that "their support was stronger the second time around because we had what they felt was a more scientifically acceptable bill." Although the APHA was widely acknowledged within the policy-making community as an ardent supporter, many informants expressed sentiments similar to the view of a staffer for a health organization that also supported the bills: "the APHA was a strong supporter, but they were not as intense as the [occupational health] nurses."

APHA: Interpretation

The APHA has a long-standing record of active involvement with progressive policies and legislation related to public health issues. As result of this tradition, the organization is typically active on behalf of several bills concerning health issues in any given congressional term. For example, in the 100th Congress (1987-88), the APHA was tracking and supporting fifteen bills in the House and Senate (including High Risk). Through its newsletter, staff members reported to the membership on how individual legislators' voting percentages on these items matched the APHA policy positions (*The Nation's Health* 1988a:7-13).

The earlier assessment of the APHA's connections via structural linkages to the public and private sectors indicated the presence of few ties to corporations. Because of the organization's membership and resource base within the public sector, it has a structural basis for independence and autonomy vis-a-vis private sector interests. At the same time, the organization also has a tradition of links to organized labor. For example, the APHA leadership has often included representatives with personal and/or professional ties to labor organizations and personnel that have the effect of predisposing the organization in favor of policy positions advocated by labor unions. As one APHA staff member commented:

> On labor union issues we largely take our cues from [APHA] sections that are very active politically on occupational safety and health and from our officers like Dr. Robbins. [Dr. Anthony Robbins, APHA President in 1983] was very sympathetic to labor union issues. So on labor union issues the organization's position is largely based on our people with the unions.[9]

In the case of the High Risk legislation, the labor union connections appear to have been influential in reinforcing the association's commitment of resources on behalf of the legislation rather than in determining the policy position. That is, as indicated earlier, the APHA policy on High Risk was consistent with long-standing policy traditions within the organization. However, the active involvement of organized labor on behalf of the legislation appeared to be instrumental in increasing the level of support the APHA devoted to the legislation. For example, an APHA staff member pointed out that when organized labor was trying to put together a coalition of labor, health, and environmental groups to support the High Risk legislation, the APHA was contacted and increased its own participation on the issue beyond what it would have been without labor's request for support. As he stated,

"We have priority level items and High Risk [was] a lower priority item [then] but [when] something was going on on the Hill with it, we raised it up."

For the APHA, ethical concerns appear to represent another motivating force underlying its support for the High Risk bills. In his 1985 testimony, Dr. Ashford addressed the ethical issues involved in risk notification: "If a Federal agency finds that worker [at risk], damn it he ought to tell the worker . . . I mean, if we are to be a fair society, we cannot avoid that responsibility. . . . [T]his bill touches upon the duty to inform" (U.S. Congress: House, 1985:273-274). The association's public policy statement on the High Risk bills also notes that there exists "[an] ethical obligation of government agencies to warn workers . . . when they are found to be at high risk [for occupational diseases]" (*American Journal of Public Health* 1987:103).

The APHA base within the public sector provides it with relative autonomy. This situation facilitates the organization's commitment to and willingness to act upon the ethical principle that workers have a right to be informed of the health risks present in the workplace, especially when that information is known and held by public agencies. The relative absence of linkages between the APHA and core actors representing the business community enhance the ability of the organization to develop a policy consistent with its commitment to ethical principles.

Evidence of the extent of this ethical commitment by the APHA to public health policies was even evident in the comments of opponents to the High Risk legislation. For example, a senior staff member within OSHA (appointed by President Reagan) observed that:

> The [American] Public Health Association came in with an idealistic perspective which was in a way kind of naive. . . . I don't question their motives at all but my experience has been that they tend to approach all issues from a purist standpoint and they don't factor in public policy implications. I think their view would be if you catch a handful of people and its good for a handful that's good enough and the other ramifications aren't considered.

The APHA's policy of support for the High Risk bills appears to have been less contingent upon contextual factors and more related to the organization's public sector membership base and its historical traditions of concern for and commitment to the protection of workers' health. Even so, the informal linkage between the association's leadership and organized labor represents an important contextual factor. The high priority assigned to the legislation by organized labor and the efforts of the AFL-CIO to mobilize organizational support for the bills clearly contributed to greater involvement by the APHA on behalf of the bills than might otherwise have occurred given the organization's relatively large legislative agenda and limited resources.

AMERICAN MEDICAL ASSOCIATION

For the 1985-86 period, no document sources could be located indicating the AMA's interest in or policy towards H.R. 1309. Interviews with senior staff members affiliated with the congressional subcommittees, the AMA, and other organizations involved with the High Risk legislation produced conflicting accounts of the AMA's position. This situation made it difficult to verify either what the AMA's position was on H.R. 1309 or if the organization was actually involved in any way with the early versions of the legislation. The absence of documents regarding AMA policy on the bill and the vague and conflicting recollections on the part of informant sources suggests either very weak or no association interest in the initial legislation.

The only archival documents expressive of the AMA's interest in and position on the High Risk legislation were two letters addressed to members of the Senate. The first letter, dated January 29, 1988, was sent to all members of the U.S. Senate and was signed by Dr. James H. Sammons, executive vice president of the AMA. In part, the letter stated that, "The American Medical Association strongly supports S.79 as reported by the Senate Labor and Human resources committee. . . . we urge passage of S.79" (U.S. Congress: Senate 1986-88). The second letter dated March 17, 1988, was addressed to Senator Metzenbaum, and was signed by Stephen C. Duffy, assistant director, Department of Congressional Affairs, AMA Washington. This letter simply restated the AMA's earlier position of support, "As the Senate moves to consider S.79" (U.S. Congress: Senate 1986-88).

The AMA's position of support for S.79 was reported to the membership via two brief notices. The first notice appeared in the organization's newsletter, *American Medical News* (1988a:8); the second reference appeared in the *Journal of the American Medical Association* (1988:2371). Aside from the letters of support, staff members from the AMA and the subcommittees confirmed that the organization also provided some limited lobbying support for the bill in the Senate in early 1988. In view of the extensive resources available to the AMA, it would appear that the activities and efforts devoted to supporting the organization's stated position of "strong support" for the High Risk legislation were rather limited.

AMA: Another View

The adjective "lukewarm" was used by several interview sources in their characterizations of the extent of AMA support for the High Risk legislation. Among both supporters and opponents of the bills, the AMA's involvement was not viewed as particularly significant. This view was based on both the timing of the decision to support the legislation and the modest political resources which the organization mobilized in support of S.79. As one congressional source put it, "an organization can support or oppose a piece of legislation at a lot of different levels. The AMA has the muscle to make things happen if it wants to. With High Risk, it didn't happen."

Despite AMA policy statements of "strong support" for the High Risk bill (S.79), various kinds of evidence suggest an actual level of support more in line with the "lukewarm" characterization. For example, informants consistently characterized the organization's lobbying efforts on behalf of the legislation as "half-hearted". Perhaps more important and illustrative of the AMA's limited commitment to the legislation is the pattern of its political action committee (American Medical Political Action Committee--AMPAC) contributions to Congressional candidates for the 1987-1988 election cycle. These data indicate a slightly *negative* relationship between the policy positions of Representatives and Senators on the High Risk legislation and the distribution of AMPAC funds. More specifically, those Senators and Representatives who had *supported* the High Risk bills in the 100th Congress and who were reelected in 1988 received a total of $847,000 in AMPAC contributions. By contrast, those who had *opposed* the legislation and who were reelected received a total of $1,016,000 in AMPAC contributions.[10] In short, political support for the High Risk bills was either not important to the distribution of AMPAC funds, or was a slightly negative factor in these decisions.

AMA: Interpretation

As the information cited in tables 5.2 and 5.3 in chapter 5 indicated, the relationship between the observed structural linkages and the AMA's policy and resource-commitment decisions was the opposite from what was expected based upon our theoretical model. The evidence related to the AMA's unexpected support for the High Risk legislation suggests the influence of a combination of contextual factors that modified the expected effects of the structural factors upon the organization's policy and resource-commitment decisions.

An important contextual factor related to the lack of fit between AMA policies on the High Risk bill and our hypothesized expectations was the size of the organization and related staff-leadership divisions. The elected, part-time board is technically the center for policy-making, but because of size, complexity, and communication gaps, the staff in such a large organization can sometimes take the lead in setting policy. This appears to have been the case in this instance. For example, interviews with a wide range of sources confirmed that the AMA's elected leadership was largely unconcerned about and uninvolved with the High Risk bills (at least until the Senate debates in early 1988). These same sources indicated that the initiation of AMA support for the legislation resulted from staff-level decisions that later provoked sharp divisions and debate among the AMA board of trustees. Some AMA senior staff members were reported to have viewed the legislation as a vehicle for improving the organization's well known "image problem" related to its "conservative" record of opposing progressive health reform legislation. To illustrate the image issue, one member of the Washington, D.C., policy-making community only half-jokingly commented that "in a sense, the AMA was way ahead of the curve; they had a 'Just Say No' policy years before Nancy [Reagan]; only for them it meant saying no to any kind of progressive health reform [legislation]."

Despite the image-angle interest in the legislation, the staff approach was to withhold endorsement of the bills until the sponsors agreed to changes that would address what one informant from a supporting health association characterized as two "parochial concerns" directly related to physicians' interests: (1) the protection of physicians from possible malpractice suits that might arise from their involvement in the medical-monitoring and job-transfer features of the legislation; (2) the exclusion from the legislation of health care workers as designated "at risk" populations--due to possible AIDS exposure hazards. It was only after these concerns were addressed in S.79, that the letter of support from the AMA's executive vice president (noted earlier) was sent to all senators in early 1988.

Returning to the issue of staff-leadership divisions, many sources confirmed that the initiation of AMA support for the High Risk legislation came as a result of contacts made by the organization's senior staff with some of the Senate sponsors of the legislation *without* the knowledge or consent of the AMA board of trustees. This action was characterized as involving a calculated understanding of the positive political consequences of what support for the legislation could have not only in terms of an image boost, but also in terms of enlarging the AMA's circle of potential political allies.

According to this latter interpretation, the AMA staff assessment was that support for the legislation would advance the organization's interests (presumably including those of the staff, leadership, and membership) in cultivating a wider set of political contacts, ties, and obligations within the Congress (especially among the more "liberal" and Democratic members). These "new bridges" (an informant's term) could be utilized at later dates on policy issues more directly related to what one informant from an organization supporting the High Risk bills characterized as the AMA's "front-burner agenda issues [such as] malpractice insurance reform and Medicare/Medicaid payment schedules."

Despite these calculated political intentions, a combination of factors complicated and undermined the ability of the staff to deploy any significant commitment of the AMA's organizational resources in support of the High Risk legislation. These factors included the corporate-sponsorship and external-corporate resource dependency patterns of the association. Also important were other linkages between many AMA officers and board members and the business community and other conservative political groups such as AMPAC and state medical PACs.[11]

The realities of close interorganizational linkages with private sector firms among physicians generally, and AMA board members specifically, were reported by AMA-based informants to have contributed to the emergence of important divisions among the policy-making leadership on the High Risk bills. As the legislation moved to the Senate, the AMA board reportedly became more conscious of the corporate drive for business unity on the legislation and of the potential consequences of the legislation for physicians as businessmen. At the same time it became clear that many of the AMA's traditional political allies in Congress were opposed to the legislation.

One important center of business opposition to the legislation was the insurance industry which had links to some AMA board members who also served as directors on the boards of insurance firms opposed to the High Risk bills (e.g., Blue Cross companies).[12] Politically, the pattern of congressional opposition to the High Risk bills led to a situation where the AMA was on the side opposite to the position taken by many of its long-time political friends and allies--such as Senator Hatch--who had served as the AMA's congressional "point man" on "Professional Liability Reform" in 1986 (U.S. Congress: Senate, 1986).

The result of this complex situation whereby the "AMA's decision" to support the High Risk legislation was made primarily at the staff level, but where interorganizational ties produced divided board interests and allegiances made strong support unlikely. As one congressional staff member opposed to the legislation put it, "the [AMA] board kind of got caught in a cross-fire." The tensions generated by the inter- and intraorganizational politics on this issue led to an outcome described by an AMA member in these terms: "Once the board found out what was going on, most of them gritted their teeth and let the policy [of public support] stand, but later, [after the bill died in the Senate] several of them raised hell about it."

It is interesting to note that the AMA, with the oldest ethical code among the seven associations,[13] never mentioned the issue of ethical principles in any of its statements of support for the High Risk legislation (i.e., the letter of support and the published reports to the membership). In fact, as one AMA member pointed out, it was economic, not ethical considerations related to the legislation that were the main concerns of rank-and-file physicians. Because many physicians are employers with health hazards in their businesses, this source pointed out that "physicians themselves would have been one of the first targets of the legislation. . . . once they realized this they said, 'We can't afford that! This [legislation] is crazy!'"

Superficially, the AMA appears to represent a case where the policy and resource-commitment decisions were inconsistent with the expectations of our theory. However, as the contextualized account of the AMA's involvement with the High Risk legislation illustrates, rather than invalidating our model, a closer examination of the organization's policy participation affirms the theory. The evidence clearly indicates that political considerations played a dominant role in generating the initial public policy position of the organization. Yet, at the same time it is also clear that important interorganizational linkages involving the leadership and the private sector eventually asserted themselves and essentially resulted in a revocation of the potential for anything other than a rather hollow, symbolic commitment on the part of the association for the legislation. This case illustrates the dynamic character of interorganizational linkages and demonstrates that while the expected influence of the posited structural ties *initially appeared* to be circumvented or neutralized, their importance was eventually asserted and they produced, albeit in a round about and partially disguised fashion, the expected effects. A full understanding of this situation requires that we consider issues over time and remain alert to the distinction between a public posture of support for legislation and the substantive commitment of resources (or lack thereof) on behalf of publicly stated policies.

AMERICAN CONFERENCE OF
GOVERNMENTAL INDUSTRIAL HYGIENISTS

Only a few documents were located that provided evidence illustrating and confirming the ACGIH's basic policy position as one of support for the High Risk legislation. The first published reference referring to the ACGIH's policy position appeared in the association's journal (*Applied Industrial Hygiene*) in May 1987, in a by-line headed: "A Message From The Chair of ACGIH" (Lee 1987:F-7). The article described an ACGIH board of directors' meeting held on March 17 and 18, 1987, where the association's policy-making process was discussed and a vote taken by the board "to endorse the High Risk Occupational Disease Notification and Prevention Act of 1987" (Lee 1987:F-7, 8). While noting that the legislation was controversial, the ACGIH chair wrote that "The Board of Directors has concluded that this Bill is now technically reasonable and feasible . . . The cost is reasonable and the Bill deserves support. The Board voted to support the resolution that, 'ACGIH supports passage of the Senate version of the High Risk Occupational Disease Notification and Prevention Act of 1987'" (Lee 1987:F-8).

The board's resolution led to the drafting of a letter of support for S.79 addressed to Senator Metzenbaum dated April 8, 1987, and signed by the ACGIH chair, Dr. Jeffrey S. Lee. In part, the letter stated, "The Board of Directors of the . . . ACGIH has voted to support passage of . . . [S.79]. . . If we can be of further assistance please do not hesitate to contact us" (*Applied Industrial Hygiene* 1987:F-24). This action was later endorsed by a membership vote conducted at the organization's annual business meeting in Montreal in May 1987 (*Applied Industrial Hygiene* 1987:F-22).

The letter of support represented the only public involvement by the ACGIH on behalf of the High Risk legislation. Following the Montreal meeting, Dr. Lee's tenure as chair ended and without his leadership on the issue, the organization was not heard from again on the High Risk legislation. Sources within the organization indicated that the letter represented the "high water mark of the organization's participation with the High Risk legislation." In part, this meant that subsequent chairs had little interest in involving the organization in what was clearly a very controversial policy issue. Given that the board of directors was reported to have been split on the vote of support for S.79, the absence of continued strong leadership support for the issue, and the lack of an organizational tradition of active involvement on public policy issues, the observed outcome of limited and transient support for the High Risk legislation is not surprising.

ACGIH: Another View

When asked about the involvement of the ACGIH with the High Risk legislation, most members of the Washington, D.C., occupational health policy and lobby community drew a blank. Informant responses ranged from "I've never heard of the organization" to "they were sort of out of the loop." Most respondents knew of the organization primarily because of the role that the ACGIH has historically played in establishing Threshold Limit Values (TLVs).[14] However, no one was aware that the association had been even marginally involved with the legislation. Even the staff of the Senate Subcommittee on Labor were unaware of the organization's 1987 letter of support, and it was not among the subcommittee file records of documents from organizations expressing support for S.79. In short, in spite of its record of limited support, the ACGIH had the lowest possible profile in terms of being recognized as supporter of the legislation within the Washington, D.C., policy-making community.

ACGIH: Interpretation

With its nonprofit sponsorship, 0 percent interpenetration, and external-nonprofit resource dependency patterns, the ACGIH *should* (according to our theory) have been a strong supporter of the High Risk legislation. In order to understand why these factors did not lead to a greater commitment of organizational resources on behalf of the legislation requires examining the influence of contextual factors in this case.

According to interview sources outside of the ACGIH, the extremely modest level of support for the legislation was partly reflective of divisions within both the organization's leadership and membership involving both economic and political considerations. Informants in organizations supportive of the High Risk legislation and aware of the ACGIH's position on the bills pointed out that the organization's leadership was especially concerned with the possible economic consequences that might occur if the ACGIH took actions strongly supportive of the High Risk bills.

To understand this interpretation, it must be noted that the ACGIH has historically cultivated a reputation as a "neutral" provider of technical informa-tion related to various aspects of industrial hygiene, including exposure standards for a wide range of toxic chemicals in the workplace [15] (i.e., TLVs). As one source put it, "the ACGIH focus has always been more on technical issues and problems." In view of this tradition, vigorous involvement by the organization on behalf of a partisan political reform effort could potentially compromise the neutral, technical image that the organization has sought to build and maintain. Political activism could, thus, have a negative effect upon the credibility of the organization, its technical publications, and *possibly* upon sales of the organization's publications--which make up an important part of its annual revenues. For example, in 1987 over $180,000 of the organization's $505,000 in total revenue was derived from "net" sales--primarily of organiza-tional publications.

Related to the potential influence of economic interests, the ACGIH case also includes indications of what might be termed "hidden interpenetration." This term refers to possible covert linkages that *could* have been important in a political sense in helping to restrain its active involvement with the High Risk legislation. Although the observed interpenetration level was 0 percent for the board of directors, the TLV Committee, historically one of the organization's most important committees, has been documented as having multiple linkages with the corporate sector (Castleman and Ziem 1988; Ziem and Castleman 1989).

No specific evidence was uncovered which demonstrated a connection between the presence of corporate representation (direct or indirect) on the TLV Committee and the organization's policy decisions concerning the High Risk legislation. However, as Castleman and Ziem have documented, over the years some ACGIH members have expressed concerns about the impact of corporate interests and representation within the TLV Committee. For example, "Dr. Hector Blejer, resigning from the Committee in 1980 after 10 years as a member, protested what he called, 'an increasingly stronger pro-industry bias . . . particularly among almost all of the Committee consultants and among the members who consult privately for private industry'" (Castleman and Ziem 1988:553).

The presence of this situation within one the organization's important committees illustrates the reality of "hidden interpenetration" and how the actions of a supposedly "neutral" committee were subject to political considerations involving the interests of industry. If this occurred within one policy-making entity of the ACGIH, it is not unreasonable to assume that the *potential* for similar political considerations existed with regard to the organization's policy towards and support for the High Risk legislation. As Castleman and Ziem (1988:554) observe: "To its discredit, the [TLV] committee has long turned a blind eye to conflicts of interest, both overt and subtle."

The reference to conflicts of interest raises the question of ethics once more. In this case we again find virtually no evidence that would indicate that the leadership's concern for ethical principles was an important factor in shaping policy and resource-commitment decisions on the High Risk legislation. Like the other cases in the study, the ACGIH has developed a code of ethics (which it shares with the AIHA [Ross 1988:F-18]). However, like the other cases, it applies to individuals, not to the organization per se. In the course of conducting interviews with informants both in and out of the ACGIH, ethical concerns were never mentioned as factors that were related to or influenced the organization's policy decisions on the High Risk legislation.

The interpretative view that ACGIH policy towards the High Risk legislation was based upon economic and/or political considerations and that it ignored ethical concerns with workers' health was disputed by the ACGIH director. In a personal communication to the author commenting on these issues, William Kelly, ACGIH executive director, maintained (1990):

> The timing of ACGIH's support for [the High Risk bill was]
> related to improvements in the feasibility of the legislation in
> accomplishing its purpose rather than anything else. The
> characterization . . . [of our support] might [best] be ex-
> pressed as "timely and appropriate.". . . To say the ACGIH
> has "cultivated the image [of neutrality]" is to infer a false
> representation of reality. . . . The discussion of the role of
> publication sales seems to be based on incomplete informa-
> tion. . . . [ACGIH's] publications contribute to public safety
> and worker health protection. . . . The ACGIH . . . is for
> worker health protection. I do not feel that it should be put
> in the box of worker exploitation on one hand or worker
> (union) political empowerment on the the other hand.

The existence of conflicting views between informants in and out of the
organization concerning the ACGIH's policy on the High Risk bills and the
factors underlying its involvement with the legislation creates a dilemma.
Which interpretation most accurately reflects the truth of the situation?
Unfortunately, there is no easy way out of this dilemma. Even so, based on
our close familiarity with the case, we would argue that the ACGIH's
involvement with and level of support for the High Risk bills was influenced
by both the posited structural linkage ties and by contextual factors with
numerous economic and political dimensions that were not fully anticipated.
The evidence indicates that the ACGIH board was divided on the High Risk
issue, but that the leadership faction endorsing the legislation was able to
prevail and provide the Senate bill with a modest, public gesture of organizational support. However, the reasons for the divisions on this issue and the
concomitant restricted level of support are less clear and are based more upon
circumstantial evidence and speculation rather than clear-cut and neatly
consistent facts. To a large extent this situation is reflective of the more
general difficulty of accessing the details of the internal and largely *nonpublic*
processes of policy discussions occurring within professional association
policy-setting boards where controversial public issues related to their
organizational interests and professional expertise are concerned.

Despite the fact that the ACGIH's involvement with the High Risk
legislation did not totally match the expectations of our model, the theory is
clearly not irrelevant in this case. On the one hand, the public sector base of
the organization appears to have predisposed at least some of its leadership
in the direction of interest in and support for the High Risk legislation. On
the other hand, the reality of a historical pattern of relatively covert corporate

involvement in the ACGIH indicates that the extent of leadership and organizational autonomy suggested by its structural linkage pattern may be partly illusory. This situation illustrates the need for greater refinement in conceptualizing, identifying, and assessing interorganizationallinkages of a sort that may be more subtle and to some extent outside of the reach of the concepts and measures utilized in this study. It also illustrates the difficulties of obtaining the data necessary for firm, evidence-based assessments of the factors that are central to policy decisions of professional societies on controversial occupational health policy legislation.

7

CASE NARRATIVES:
THREE WHO PASSED

In our profession we are, again I will repeat, professional
people and we are not interested whatsoever with economics.
We are interested in the health of the working man and this
is precisely what we adhere to.

> Testimony of George D. Clayton, Executive Secre-
> tary, AIHA, OSH Act Hearings. U.S. Congress:
> Senate, 1969, p. 181.

The format of this chapter is identical to chapter 6 except here we present
information related to the policy and resource-commitment decisions of the
three associations which were either neutral towards or opposed to the High
Risk legislation. Each narrative sketch follows the same three section format
used in chapter 6.

AMERICAN SOCIETY OF SAFETY ENGINEERS

A review of the ASSE journal (*Professional Safety*) from 1985 through
1989 revealed virtually no references to the High Risk legislation. The only
explicit listing was a one-sentence comment: "Workplace health, safety topics
to watch in '89 . . . Worker Risk Notification. Expect renewed action on two
fronts: renewed efforts to legislate a notification program, and continued work
by the National Institute for Occupational Safety and Health to establish a
notification program of its own" (*Professional Safety* 1989b:33). While widely
scattered references to the organization's general interests in occupational
health and safety policies were evident, there were no other indications of
association interest in or comment on the High Risk legislation in its journal.

In an interview, an ASSE staff member responsible for legislative affairs
commented on the noninvolvement of the association with the High Risk

legislation: "We've never been involved with that and as far as I know, we've never taken a position on it." Even though the evidence does indicate a stance of neutrality and noninvolvement on the part of the ASSE with the High Risk legislation, the organization was active in governmental affairs and public policy related to other occupational health and safety issues during the 1985-88 period. For example, when a candidate favored by the ASSE was being considered for appointment to the Department of Labor, the organization mounted a "nationwide letter campaign . . . [supporting] the confirmation . . . [of] ASSE member John Pendergrass . . . as Assistant Secretary of Labor for OSHA" (*Professional Safety* 1986:14).

ASSE: Another View

As the High Risk legislation was being prepared in late 1984 and early 1985, informal contacts were initiated by Democratic staff members of the House Subcommittee on Health and Safety with the ASSE's leadership. These conversations indicated that the ASSE leadership intended to remain neutral and not involve the organization in the development of the legislation. As one congressional staff member stated:

> Their sense was that since the bill did nothing in terms of regulatory aspects requiring engineering designs to reduce exposures, they didn't consider it appropriate for them to become involved and speak on disease exposures or medical monitoring. Their emphasis is on engineering designs like ventilation systems and things like that which would preclude exposures to begin with. So they stayed out of the picture.

Additional interviews with a variety of other members of the policy-making community, including supporters and opponents of the High Risk legislation, confirmed the aloofness and apparent neutrality of the ASSE on this issue. As one union-based supporter of the legislation stated "they were never heard from in this case."

ASSE: Interpretation

The ASSE's structural linkage pattern indicates strong, multiple ties with the private sector. On the basis of our model, such connections should have been associated with strong, negative involvement on the part of the ASSE. Despite the absence of such clear-cut results in this case, a qualitative review and interpretation of the evidence related to the ASSE's position indicates that the apparent inconsistency between the theoretical expectations and the observed outcomes are not as disparate as they might appear on the surface. As we noted in chapter 1, an association position of neutrality on policy issues can be legitimately interpreted as a *de facto* position of opposition. Thus, from this perspective, the basic ASSE policy of neutrality on the High Risk legislation is not inconsistent with the expectations of the theory. Also, a recurring feature of professional associations which helps us to understand trends and preferences in the policy views and interests of the ASSE is the reality of overlapping interests and activities with other associations. In the case of the ASSE, the organization participates in various activities that link it with other associations with occupational health and safety interests including the AIHA--which was a strong opponent of the legislation.

As an illustration of the ASSE-AIHA connections, a report in the ASSE journal pointed out that the organization was a participant in "the first meeting of the Intersociety Forum, a group uniting all safety and health professional societies. . . . In January, 1974 . . . the ASSE [participated in] an Intersociety Conference sponsored by the AIHA" (*Professional Safety* 1986:14). Also, the leadership of the ASSE and the AIHA have worked together on common projects including a joint effort related to the appointment of a new OSHA director in 1985:

> AIHA President Howard L. Kusnetz and ASSE President Delmar E. Talley recognize a similarity of interests and have contacted Secretary of Labor William E. Brock, urging him to select an assistant secretary whose background reflects extensive safety and industrial hygiene knowledge. . . . Both presidents have offered the resources of their organizations to help with the search (*Professional Safety* 1985:8).

The intersection of the ASSE's leadership and activities with those of the AIHA are clear. This linkage combined with the past record of ASSE policy on the original OSH Act (Page and O'Brien 1973:151) suggests that although the organization may have been neutral on the High Risk legislation, its interests and sympathies were clearly with the corporate sector. The fact that the legislation did not directly address safety issues was viewed by some informants as a convenient rationale which the organization used as a justification for remaining aloof. Supporters of the legislation generally agreed with the observation of a union-based informant who acknowledged that the ASSE was "not a player in the High Risk [case], but everybody knows they're all corporate guys."

In 1988 the ASSE positioned the issue of ethics on page one of its journal (*Professional Safety* 1988:1). In the same issue, the "President's Editorial" addressed the topic of "Professional Ethics" (Ibid:4); the organization's code of ethics was also included in the issue for reference (Ibid:53). The reasons for explicitly addressing ethics at this time were not made clear. However, what is clear is that, as was the case with the other associations, when the issue of ethics is broached, it is almost always addressed in individualistic terms.   That is, ethical conduct on the part of individual members is encouraged, but the same standards are virtually never applied by the association's leadership to the organization's involvement in public issues. Thus, in the case of the High Risk legislation, the issue of ethics was never mentioned or noted by the ASSE or any informants as relevant in any way to the organization's policy of noninvolvement.

The ASSE's structural linkage pattern and the evidence illustrative of overlapping interests with the AIHA indicates that the decision to remain neutral on the High Risk legislation was both easy and convenient for the association.   In 1985, the core actors representing the business community were united in their opposition to the High Risk legislation. Corporate opposition to the High Risk legislation was especially strong in the insurance industry--where the ASSE has strong historical roots and leadership connections. Indeed, the 1987 board of directors and officers included at least five members who were executive officers (vice presidents) of large insurance companies.[1] The association's close connections with the business community and its ties to outspoken opponents of the High Risk legislation among professional groups (such as the AIHA), leave little doubt where the organization's sympathies lay in this case.[2]

AMERICAN OCCUPATIONAL MEDICAL ASSOCIATION

The AOMA maintained a posture of public neutrality throughout the political struggles over the High Risk bills. The organization's "Association Affairs" feature in various issues of the *Journal of Occupational Medicine* during 1985 includes no references to the High Risk legislation. There were also no references to the legislation in the *Journal* during 1986, 1987, or 1988. However, research articles referring to risk notification projects and issues did appear in the *Journal* during the 1985-86 period (Schulte et al. 1985; Tillett et al. 1986; Ruttenberg and Powers 1986).

The publicly neutral posture of the association was emphasized by an AOMA staff member: "we were neutral on the legislation and weren't formally involved with it." However, coexisting with public assertions of neutrality were indications of both interest and involvement by the association's leadership--at informal levels. For example, congressional staffers confirmed that informal meetings were held between officers of the organization and staff members from the House Health and Safety Subcommittee as early as 1985. These informal contacts were apparently maintained over the entire period that the bill was being considered in the House. Evidence of a continuing informal dialogue between congressional policy makers and the AOMA's leadership is found in a letter from the president of the AOMA, Dr. T. Forrest Fisher, addressed to Congressman Gaydos on April 21, 1987. The letter followed a meeting in Washington, D.C., which involved Dr. Fisher, Dr. James L. Craig (president of the American Academy of Occupational Medicine), and senior staff members of the House Health and Safety Subcommittee. In part, the letter stated that "the most recent changes in the substitute version [of H.R. 162] certainly enhance the value of the bill. . . . I appreciate the opportunity to contribute and participate with [the committee]" (U.S. Congress: House 1985-88). Copies of the letter were distributed to the other AOMA officers. Thus, it is clear that while the AOMA may have been publicly neutral, the organization's leadership was personally involved in monitoring the legislation and in providing input concerning proposed modifications to the bills as they moved through the Congress.

AOMA: Another View

Within the Washington, D.C., policy-making community, the interests and involvement of the AOMA leadership with the High Risk legislation were widely recognized. Most sources emphasized the connections between the association and corporations. As one trade association staff member put it, "they remained neutral, but a lot of their members were opposed to it." Despite the fact that the AOMA was widely viewed as sympathetic to business interests, none of the interviews provided any evidence that the organization had been an active, *public* force against the High Risk legislation. Those informants critical of the organization were mainly concerned about the apparent conflict of interest in terms of corporate loyalties versus physician loyalties to workers as patients.

AOMA: Interpretation

The structural linkage pattern and policy decisions associated with AOMA are virtually identical to those of the ASSE. Like the ASSE, AOMA also adopted a public stance of neutrality on the High Risk legislation. As was the case with the ASSE, we argue that the meaning and purpose of neutrality as a policy choice can be understood as a *de facto* position of opposition to the legislation. (Recall Miller from chapter one who points out that "by taking no position the societies, in effect, take a very influential position" [1972:249]).

A variety of informants indicated that the adoption of a formally neutral position on the High Risk bills by the AOMA leadership represented, at least in part, a means of avoiding conflicts with corporate "sponsor-patrons" while simultaneously maintaining a public *appearance* of scientific objectivity. Of course, a position of neutrality sidesteps any need to consider decisions concerning the commitment of organizational resources. In this case, by choosing to not take a position the AOMA policy had the net effect of reinforcing the status quo. This meant, in this instance, the perpetuation of continued serious, negative health effects for workers as a partial consequence of the inaction of the organization. Viewed from this interpretive perspective, the policy decision of neutrality adopted by the AOMA and the concomitant lack of any need for resource commitments concerning the High Risk legislation suggests the decision outcomes were not as inconsistent with the expectations of our model as they might appear to be.

The issue of ethics is one that occupational physicians have become increasingly sensitive to since the passage of the OSH Act resulted in greater scrutiny of the interests and activities of physicians who are employed by private corporations. As Berman (1978:98) notes, "As a response to public criticism of occupational medicine, company physicians have begun to defend themselves in professional journals." In 1976, the AOMA adopted a code of ethics and published it on the cover of its journal (*Journal of Occupational Medicine* 1976). Despite this public commitment to ethical principles, researchers addressing this issue find that for the most part, company physicians tend to identify their interests with those of their employers and see no ethical conflicts (e.g., Brodeur 1974:243-244; Walters 1982, 1985; Walsh 1987:139-173).

In the case of the High Risk legislation, the relationship between ethical principles and AOMA's policies on legislative issues was never addressed in any of the organization's publications. Of course, this situation is not inconsistent with the other cases, nor is it surprising. The reality of closely interwoven linkages with corporate employers and resource providers appears to impose severe constraints on the organization's autonomy. By this we refer to the ability and/or willingness of the leadership to commit the *organization* to policy positions on legislation that would be consistent with the ethical principles to which the individual members are publicly committed to uphold.[3]

Although the AOMA's public stance was one of neutrality, there are indications that *informally* the organization's position was one of opposition to the legislation. In an interview, an AOMA staff member's remarks suggested how this situation was possible:

We are small and so we don't have lobbyists in Washington to be putting forth our message and so we really rely on individuals who are coming in and wearing different hats. They might come in representing the American Petroleum Institute because they happen to work for an oil company when they are also members of ours and they're stating things that are really for both associations. At any given time they can be representing two or three different factions but I think they're all pretty much together on thinking on High Risk. That's why you don't see testimony coming directly from us because we do not have a political arm.

The view that the organization was a covert opponent of the legislation and that the ties between the leadership and industry compromised the ethics espoused by the organization was bluntly expressed by an AFL-CIO staff member: "They don't know what they want. On the one hand, they're doctors and they're supposed to have some professional responsibility to medicine. On the other hand, the corporations pay their wages and when push came to shove, they sided with the corporations [and opposed] the bills."

For the AOMA, a public position of neutrality on the High Risk legislation offered the organization the means for resolving a difficult dilemma. That is, the bills confronted the organization with an issue that juxtaposed the professional ideals of ethics, service, and client advocacy with the realities of interorganizational resource linkages involving extensive interpenetration with corporate management structures and a pattern of extensive resource dependency upon corporate resources. Public neutrality permitted the organization to avoid the appearance of bias. However, as we have seen, an interpretative account of the organization's involvement with the legislation makes it clear that the policy outcomes were not at odds with the theoretically based expectations.

AMERICAN INDUSTRIAL HYGIENE ASSOCIATION

On November 2, 1985, the AIHA President, Howard L. Kusnetz, received a request "from Congressman Gaydos for the AIHA to testify [on H.R. 1309] on November 13" (Kusnetz 1986a:A-72). This short notice forced the organization to move swiftly in order "to have 35 copies of the testimony in the Congressional Committee's hands by Friday, November 8" (Ibid). In six days the AIHA's executive and law committees were able to agree on a position and prepare a document for the hearing. The president of the AIHA succinctly stated the organization's position on H.R. 1309: "In short, we opposed the bill" (Ibid).

The testimony of the AIHA was presented to the House Health and Safety Subcommittee hearing on November 13, 1985, by the organization's treasurer, Joseph Holtshouser (accompanied by the AIHA Law Committee chairman, Roy Deitchman). The testimony involved objections to several portions of the bill; in an oral statement, Mr. Holtshouser summed up the AIHA's objections to the bill:

> No. 1, we don't feel that it has been demonstrated enough need for House rule 1309 . . . No.2, the approach envisioned . . . with regard toward the application of epidemiology is technically faulty. No.3, mechanism (sic) for communication to employees are in place and about to be expanded ([the OSHA Hazard Communication Standard]). They should be given the opportunity to be applied" (U.S. Congress: House, 1985:373).

Following the AIHA's negative testimony on H.R. 1309, the organization experienced an episode of internal dissent which appeared to temper the leadership's activities and positions regarding later versions of the High Risk bills. Although membership expressions of disagreement with the AIHA's policy position on H.R. 1309 did not appear to produce changes in the organization's basic position of opposition, subsequent association testimony on later bills indicates that the association leadership appeared to have moderated its opposition to the legislation.

In the hearings on S.79 in February 1987, by the Senate Subcommittee on Labor, the AIHA provided a prepared statement but did not send a representative to present testimony to the subcommittee. The prepared statement was very similar to the one which the organization later submitted to the House Subcommittee on Health and Safety at its hearings in March 1987, on H.R. 162. The position outlined was essentially negative with regard to S.79. However, in a cover letter accompanying the prepared testimony, the AIHA president, Alice C. Farrar, hinted that the organization had moved away from its 1985 position of strong opposition to the High Risk legislation: "The Association supports the goals and several provisions of this bill. . . . Strengthening the legal requirement for employee notification will help us . . . improve the health and safety protection services for Americans at work" (U.S. Congress: Senate, 1987a:301-302).

In March 1987, Dr. William Popendorf, secretary of the AIHA board of directors testified for the organization before the House Health and Safety Subcommittee on H.R. 162. The essential thrust of the testimony was one of opposition to the new version of the High Risk bill. However, there were hints that the organization's position was perhaps open to compromise and accommodation. For example, in his oral testimony, Dr. Popendorf stated: "I think if the constraints were built in to make it a reasonable program . . . we would agree that it is a beneficial program and we could support its implementation" (U.S. Congress: House, 1987a:152-153).

AIHA: Another View

The position of the AIHA of opposition to the High Risk bills was not surprising to informants in Washington, D.C., who were regular participants in or observers of the occupational health policy-making process. For the most part, there was a clear awareness of the links between the AIHA and the interests of industry on the High Risk issue. Throughout the 1985-88 period while the High Risk legislation was being considered and developed, the AIHA was known and referred to as "a consistent opponent of the legislation" by several informants. Among senior Democratic congressional staff members, there was a consensus that the AIHA "represented corporate interests."

At one juncture in the 1987 House testimony, Congressman Gaydos pointed up AIHA-industry linkages and interests in a series of questions to Dr. Popendorf concerning the AIHA's membership and finances: Mr. Gaydos (speaking): "I do not see [in your statement] how you run your business. Could you tell me? I mean, where do you raise your money, how do you keep together? Who finances you?" (U.S. Congress: House, 1987a:146). In response to Congressman Gaydos' questions, Dr. Popendorf described some of the revenue-raising activities of the association, its policy-making process for developing positions on legislative issues, and the membership composition. During a description of the organization's membership, Congressman Gaydos raised two questions that highlighted the AIHA's connections with industry interests: Mr. Gaydos (speaking): "And again, just for emphasis, you say the Association has approximately 7,000 members, right?" Mr. Popendorf (speaking): "Yes Sir." Mr. Gaydos (speaking): "And about two-thirds employed in the private sector . . . right?" Mr. Popendorf (speaking): "Yes Sir. That's Right" (U.S. Congress: House, 1987a:147).

AIHA: Interpretation

The structural linkage subtypes and policy decisions observed for the AIHA represent an example of an invariant pattern that is consistent with the expectations of our theory. Even so, the participation of the AIHA in the development of the High Risk legislation was also influenced by contextual factors which, in this case, involved a significant episode of internal dissent. This event appeared to modify the organization's initial policy position and later participation in the legislative process.

Following the organization's testimony in 1985, the AIHA leadership was confronted by membership dissent from what the association's president seemed to indicate was a distinct minority within the organization: "Most people who contacted me after the testimony was presented . . . were in agreement with our position" (Kusnetz 1986a:A-72). It is difficult to know the extent of the internal disagreement among the membership regarding the AIHA position on H.R. 1309, but it is clear that it was sufficient to cause the organization's leadership to publicly address it and later to take steps to change the policy-making process. Sources close to this issue indicated that the internal dissent was primarily centered within and led by AIHA members employed in public sector positions--as would be expected by our theory.

Dissenting commentary was registered through letters which appeared in at least three different forums. These included a letter to Congressman Gaydos dated January 7, 1986, and signed by sixteen members of the AIHA, a partially published letter to the AIHA president from a former OSHA official (Kusnetz March 1986a:A-72), and a third letter that appeared in the "Letters To The Editor" feature in the March 1986 issue of the *American Industrial Hygiene Association Journal*. The letter to Congressman Gaydos was appended to the 1985 subcommittee hearing record and in part stated, "In summary, we want to go on record in support of H.R. 1309, with some modifications, and to deplore the action of the AIHA in testifying against the Bill" (U.S. Congress: House, 1985:520). (A copy of the letter was also sent to Mr. Holtshouser.)

The effects of this internal dissent upon the AIHA leadership appeared to be manifested in at least three different ways. First, there was an immediate public statement in the AIHA journal essentially justifying the position that was taken by the organization on H.R. 1309 (Kusnetz 1986a: A-72; 1986b: A-136). Second, a longer-term effect involved a revision by the AIHA's board of directors in October 1986 of the procedures to be followed by the AIHA in "taking public positions on issues of concern to the membership and the profession" (Farrar 1987:A-234). In April 1987, the AIHA board of directors adopted a revised version of the October 1986 policy document and published it as "The AIHA Public Positions Procedure" (*American Industrial Hygiene Association Journal* 1987a:A-420). The third effect of the internal dissent appeared to be one of softening the AIHA's opposition to the High Risk bills in the 100th Congress.

Some senior congressional subcommittee staff members detected a slight change in the organization's position in 1987 as compared with 1985. As one staffer put it, "they were less negative in '87 than they were in '85." This shift was ascribed both to the internal dissent over the legislation and also to the split within the business community over the legislation. In interviews where the latter factor was brought up, one congressional informant pointed out:

> As a result of changes in the bills, the business community started to split. And since many of the industrial hygienists who are leaders in the [AIHA] work for various businesses, some worked for businesses that supported the legislation and some worked for businesses that opposed the bills. So they couldn't come to as much resolution internally and instead of taking a position in '87, they talked more about the feasibilities, technical, and operative sections of the bills.

Although the AIHA remained opposed to the High Risk bills throughout the 1985-88 period, the evidence indicates that its opposition did not involve an extensive commitment of organizational resources in support of this policy position. For example, no documentary evidence was found or reported by informants indicative of any active lobbying efforts against the bills on the part of the AIHA throughout this time period.

The links between AIHA policy on the High Risk legislation and ethics were at best indirect. The internal dissent within the AIHA over the High Risk legislation was partly focused upon ethical concerns and issues. For example, the letter which dissident AIHA members addressed to Congressman Gaydos stated in part that "We see its potential. . . to advance the principle of workers' rights to information about the risks they face on the job" (U.S. Congress: House, 1985:519).

Like the other organizations in the study, the AIHA has adopted a code of ethics (jointly with the ACGIH: *American Industrial Hygiene Association Journal* 1987b:A-546). However, as in most of the other cases, it is explicitly individualistic in its focus. It includes no provisions that obligate the organization to act in accordance with the ethical principles that are binding upon individual members. Although the issue of ethics was touched upon by those AIHA members who disagreed with a policy of opposition to the legislation, the organizational leadership did not address the topic in any of its congressional appearances or public comments on the legislation. This lack of attention to ethical concerns on policy issues is neither unusual nor surprising--especially given the AIHA's strong, multiple corporate ties. However, in addition to the observed structural linkage pattern for this organization, the AIHA also has a unique membership profile that further inhibits its autonomy and ability to act on the basis of ethical principles on policy issues involving conflicting labor-business interests. In addition to its approximately 7,000 individual members, the AIHA also includes "over 440 organizational members from industry and closely allied areas" (Cralley 1988:482). This means that in 1987, approximately 88 percent of the AIHA's organizational members were private sector firms.[4] In short, for the AIHA, as was the case with most of the other associations, the omission of any statements of concern for ethical principles by the leadership where organizational policies were concerned indicates that such issues were not viewed as relevant to the association's position on the High Risk legislation. This lack of concern for ethics at the organizational level is hardly surprising given the close and extensive connections between the AIHA and industry.

In an earlier study, the AIHA was included as one of what Berman referred to as the "captive specialties" (1978:94). The evidence presented here illustrates the nature and extent of the structural linkages and other relationships between the AIHA and the corporate sector and tends to support such a characterization. However, as this case also illustrates, even in the absence of the structural prerequisites for organizational autonomy, contextual events and circumstances can exert a modifying influence upon the policy positions adopted by even the most captive organization. Of course, it must also be pointed out that the ability of the dissident group to have an effect was linked to the gradual transformation of the AIHA's membership base (since the passage of the OSH Act) away from a position of virtual dominance by corporate sector employers to a recent, rapid expansion in members employed in the public sector. This shift provided dissidents with the numbers and relatively autonomous base necessary to mount a challenge against the corporate-dominated leadership.

8

SUMMARY AND CONCLUSIONS

[The] current interest in researching the relationship between work and cancer . . . is due to a large degree to working class and the general population's outcry on the damage being created at the work-place. But still, the hegemony which the bourgeoisie has in all scientific institutions explains the nature and bias of that response, a bias reflected in the choice of areas to be researched and the means and ways of researching it. . . . In this respect, the [health] scientist is, to use a Gramscian term, an organic intellectual of the bourgeoisie who explains the reality with and for the bourgeoisie. This relationship of scientist/bourgeoisie is overwhelmingly clear in the United States where most research is sponsored either by private foundations or by the state where capital's representatives are extremely powerful and influential.

> Vicente Navarro, *Crisis, Health, and Medicine*, 1986, pp. 171-172.

ON NEGLECTING WORKERS AND REPORTING THE OBVIOUS

In 1989, the three television networks devoted a total of "just a little over 13 minutes the entire year for [occupational] safety and health stories" (Tasini 1990:28). In the same year, out of 1,000 evening news broadcasts by the three major networks, "little more than 2% of total air time went to *all* workers' issues" (Cockburn 1991:17). The indications are that unless workers' organizations press for changes, "labor issues [will continue to be] ignored by [the] corporate owned media" (Harvey 1991:20). The pattern of media neglect of occupational health and safety concerns also extends to the policy arena as well. This point was underscored by a senior congressional staff member's comments in late 1989:

You know, I can think back to the hundreds of hearings that
we have conducted in our subcommittee . . . in the last five
years.   Only once did we have a significant number of
general media--and when I say general media I mean like
television stations and the *New York Times*, or *Washington
Post* or *Wall Street Journal*--come to our hearings . . . and
that was on what happened in Bophal [India].   Everybody
came. Well, we did the follow-up hearing two months later
on what was going on in Institute, West Virgina, where this
stuff [(isocyanide)] was also being made. [We] had the trade
press and nobody else came by. And that is very typical. We
do not have and have never been able to generate a great
deal of public interest in occupational safety and health.

At the same time that workers' issues are ignored, the mass media
continues to portray scientists in objective terms. Media reports typically
imply that scientists and professionals lack political biases, hidden agendas, or
compromising links to organizations with direct interests in reforms on
important and controversial policy issues. For example, in a recent *New York
Times* story contrasting the views of the auto industry with those of environmental groups on questions of auto safety and economy, the following
statement is offered as a means of reconciling competing positions: "Most
lawmakers lack the technical expertise to evaluate which side is right, so the
Department of Transportation has enlisted a committee of the National
Academy of Sciences to determine what standards are technically and
economically feasible" (Levin 1991:37). The clear implication is that scientists
are informed but disinterested parties without political or ideological biases.
This means they can be trusted to use their neutral, scientific expertise to
resolve complex policy issues on the basis of science, not politics.

Our data indicate that for the most part, associations of health and safety
professionals are hardly disinterested or unbiased where occupational health
policy reforms are concerned. As a result, most of these organizations are not
likely to be in the vanguard of legislative reform efforts on this issue. The
documentation of the reasons for the failure of most professional societies to
take an activist stance on what is clearly a major public health crisis has been
a central feature of this study. Despite claims of commitments to public
service and ethical ideals, our evidence on interorganizational linkages suggests substantial grounds for remaining circumspect where the interests and
allegiances of these organizations are concerned.

To some observers, the information we have presented may seem to be
rather unsurprising news.[1] However, it is our view that what may appear as
obvious to some groups cannot be assumed to be obvious to everyone. In

light of the continuing media neglect of occupational health and safety issues along with the simultaneous portrayal of scientists as neutral arbitrators in policy disputes, we believe that we must pay close attention to the detailed reality of how and why professional groups participate as they do in the policy reform process. The factors that compromise or facilitate the autonomy of these groups must be identified, documented, and reported (over and over again if need be) in order to delineate in the clearest possible terms the gap between cultural ideals and political realities where professional associations' policies on occupational health policy reforms are concerned.

CASE NARRATIVES AND HYPOTHESES: A RECONSIDERATION

The case narratives presented in chapters 6 and 7 include important facts and insights related to the role of contextual factors in shaping association policy decisions in the High Risk case. In view of this information, it is useful to briefly reconsider our research hypotheses in order to assess more directly the extent to which contextual factors influenced the hypothesized effects of the structural linkage factors. Accordingly, we turn briefly to a review of our hypotheses, data from the case narratives, and our theoretical model.

The Research Hypotheses Revisited

The analysis developed in chapter 5 indicated that the structural linkage patterns and basic policy and resource-commitment decisions of the AAOHN and AMA presented some problems for our theory. The AMA was especially problematic because of the inconsistency between its sponsorship and resource dependency linkages to the corporate sector and its basic policy position of support for the legislation. Even so, as the AMA case narrative illustrated, political considerations involving internal policy decisions of the AMA staff and the reality of the AMA board members' linkages to external corporate interests were shown to produce a kind of dual-level policy outcome. The policy of public support by the AMA for the legislation remained in place, but board opposition prevented any meaningful commitment of organizational resources on behalf of the policy. In short, the AMA case illustrates how staff-generated association public policy statements can be vitiated by leadership opposition and the concomitant withholding of organizational resources on behalf of publicly stated policies. This interpretative account of the AMA's policy on the legislation makes it clear that the effects of its structural linkages to the corporate sector did *eventually* produce policy decisions in the directions predicted by our model. What was missed by our theory was the *timing* of the eventual policy outcomes and the complication of the case by what could be viewed as unanticipated contextual factors. These included the reality and importance of staff-board divisions on policy issues as well as the influence of informal communication channels and shifting political circumstances. Thus, while the structural linkages did finally exert their expected effects upon AMA policy, the influence of this cluster of unanticipated contextual factors complicated the outcome.

The AAOHN case was less problematic. For this organization the policy and resource-commitment decisions were generally consistent with the expectations of our theory. However, the AAOHN case narrative also makes it clear that the partial presence of structural linkage subtypes that were expected to produce supportive effects were reinforced by a kind of contextual factor unanticipated by our theory, viz, the association's "professionalization project." This factor was certainly important in producing a resource-commitment level beyond what would have been expected on the basis of the observed structural linkage pattern alone.

The ACGIH exhibited an invariant "positive" structural linkage pattern and also supported the High Risk legislation. Superficially anyway, this case appears to offer support for our first hypothesis and for our theory generally. While a policy of support did obtain publicly, the case narrative suggests that the effects of the structural linkages upon the organization's resource-commitment level were modified by the existence of contextual factors related to economic and political considerations. In this respect, the case narrative illustrates how contextual factors may act as "intervening variables" in tempering the expected effects of structural linkages upon resource-commitment levels.

The APHA exhibited an invariant "positive" structural linkage pattern and also strongly supported the High Risk legislation. As a result, this case offers support for both of our hypotheses and the expectations of our theory generally. Even so, the case narrative also points out the APHA is atypical in that the expected effects of the structural linkages were reinforced by the existence of informal linkages with core actors representing organized labor. The relative autonomy of the organization (vis-a-vis the corporate sector) appears to make possible not only the cultivation of such ties with labor, but also the ability of the leadership to endorse policies that are explicitly concerned and consistent with ethical principles and commitments at the organizational level. As the case narratives illustrate, the APHA was the only organization that exhibited this latter characteristic.

Among associations adopting neutral or opposed policies to the High Risk legislation, both the ASSE and AOMA exhibited invariant "negative" structural linkage patterns indicative of strong ties to the corporate sector. For these two organizations, the case narratives reinforce the hypothesis that the observed structural linkages would produce neutral or opposed policy outcomes. At the same time, the narratives also make the point that the organizations' resource-commitment levels only *trended* in the direction expected by our second hypothesis. These levels were not nearly as strong as expected given their strong corporate connections.

The value of the narratives in these two cases is that they allow us to look more closely at how contextual factors were important in modifying the expected effects of the structural linkages. For example, although the ASSE and AOMA adopted neutral policies on the legislation, the narratives provide information indicative of *informal opposition* to the High Risk bills. This outcome places the results much closer to the expectations of the theory. The evidence for this conclusion was stronger for the AOMA than for the ASSE, but in both cases the narratives offer additional support for the expected effects of multiple, negative structural linkages upon the policies of these organizations. At the same time, the narratives illustrate how contextual factors (for AOMA, concern for ethical appearances and for ASSE, perceived relevance) muted or mitigated the expected effects of their strong corporate ties upon their legislative policy decisions.

The AIHA's invariant "negative" structural linkage pattern and its policy of opposition supports our first hypothesis. For the most part, the details provided in the case narrative add support for the hypothesized effects of the structural linkages upon the organization's resource-commitment levels as well. The initial stance of active opposition by the AIHA leadership to the High Risk bills in 1985 illustrates the expected influence of its linkages to the corporate sector. However, at the same time, the emergence of internal dissent within the AIHA, the 1987 split in the business community, and the moderation of AIHA opposition to the High Risk bills in 1987 illustrate how contextual factors in the internal and external environments can produce modifying effects upon organizational policies--even for one with very strong corporate ties.

RECURRING ISSUES AND THEMES

In chapter 1 we outlined three major issues that guided the inquiry and which also were at the core of the more general objectives of the book. In the following sections we reconsider these issues and assess the extent to which the study advances our stated purposes for considering them and our understanding of the sociological implications associated with them. These sections also revisit a theme introduced in chapter 1, viz, the tension between the

ideals and realities. Promise versus performance. In this instance, it refers to the question: Have we accomplished what we set out to do?

Health Policy and Health Politics

Our results add to a growing body of literature based upon a multidimensional view of the meaning of health policy. In many respects the growth of such an orientation represents a renewed interest in health and health policy issues within the framework of what has historically been known as "social medicine."[2] This tradition locates the sources of health and disease within social, economic, and political structures, relationships, and organizations (e.g., Sigerist 1941, 1943; Rosen 1948, 1974; Navarro 1976, 1983, 1985, 1986; Waitzkin 1983; Silver 1984).

Occupational health is an especially important dimension of health policy within the social medicine tradition. As early as the mid-1800s, the proponents of social medicine recognized "that the provision of medical care was not enough . . . it must go hand in hand with social prophylaxis. . . . To deal with [these issues] Leubuscher, [a nineteenth-century advocate of social medicine], proposed a program of industrial hygiene, with emphasis on the legislative regulation of working conditions" (Rosen 1974:69). The views of various contemporary health and medical researchers who share many of the basic ideas of the social medicine tradition reflect similar policy concerns: "We have not been sufficiently cognizant that health policy is also embodied in . . . employment policies [and] . . . the occupational environment" (Levine and Lilienfeld 1987:5-6). "The detection, prevention, and treatment of occupational disease must be integrated into the overall health care system" (Coye et al. 1984:101).

With its explicit focus upon the High Risk legislation as one facet of a broad, social medicine-style conceptualization of health policy, this study illustrates how occupational health policy concerns transcend the notion that such matters are "merely labor issues." Framing risk notification within the context of the links between workplace exposures to hazardous substances, patterns of health outcomes as well as economic and political consequences clearly illuminates how and why the High Risk legislation represents an integral element of a multidimensional approach to health policy. This perspective encourages an expansion of traditional views of the meaning of national health policy to include a comprehensive array of complementary programs focusing not only upon the provision of health services, but also upon primary and secondary disease prevention--both in an out of the workplace.

The evidence we presented also contributes to a better understanding of how and why health policy reforms which include health-protective, disease-- prevention features (such as the High Risk legislation) involve more than merely technical and scientific questions and concerns. It illustrates how and why such proposals are laced with political implications and consequences for a wide range of interested groups and organizations. The High Risk legislation makes the political aspects of occupational health policy formulation especially obvious. It highlights how the political divisions and conflicts related to the occupational dimension of health policy tend to be based upon class-like conflicts and related coalitional formations centered around core actor organizations linked to business and labor.

The Politics of Redistributive Policies

Where health politics are concerned, we have shown how the intensity of political conflicts related to developing occupational health policy are directly linked to the extent to which these policy issues involve redistributive features. As noted earlier, while the High Risk legislation was much more modest than the OSH Act in terms of its scope and effects, it was, nevertheless, viewed by the business community as representing a similar kind of economic and ideological and/or political threat to corporate interests. The latter dimension, while less directly tangible than the redistributive material dimension of the High Risk legislation is, as we have shown, also very important to the politics of occupational health reform. Our findings concerning the conflicted politics of the High Risk bills illustrate and echo a sentiment expressed by Calavita in an earlier study of the symbolic ideological and political significance of the OSH Act for both labor and business: "symbolic action . . . may significantly modify *ideological* conditions, by telling workers: . . . 'The most important lesson is that you can win'" (Calavita 1983:446).

We have shown that the conflicted politics of occupational health policy reform leads to efforts by both core actor groups to recruit political allies from various peripheral groups, including professional associations. Moreover, we have also shown how corporate organizations have a structural advantage over labor organizations in the political struggles to mobilize and/or neutralize professional societies. The multiple linkages that exist between many professional associations and the business community have been constructed and cultivated over extended periods of time and tie large segments of their members and leaders to the ideological perspective and material interests of the corporate sector. Such an arrangement obviously places labor at a decided political disadvantage when it comes to recruiting political support for occupational health policy reforms from among health and safety professional groups.

To the extent that health policy is reconceptualized in terms of the interdependent dimensions of prevention and health services and includes programs with both health protection and health service provisions, then the politics of health policy reform are likely to become increasingly conflicted. This means that policies such as risk notification, which emphasize health-protective, disease-prevention measures and provisions (extending *beyond* lifestyle and health-promotion features) cause the health policy formation process to shift increasingly in the direction of redistributive-styles of political conflicts and coalitions. As we have shown, health policy reforms such as the High Risk legislation which mandate health protection programs raise the stakes insofar as policy outcomes are concerned (especially for the core organizational actors) and make the health policy process extremely contentious. Under these conditions, interorganizational linkages become especially important in shaping the formation of political coalitions among organizations with direct interests in the content of health policy reforms and their outcomes.

Ethics, Interests, Autonomy, and Policy

In the first chapter it was noted that little is known about the influence of ethical codes and ideals upon the behavior of professionals. While we did not directly address that issue at the level of individual practitioners, we did address it at the organizational level via two central concerns. First we focused upon a direct consideration of the structural bases of organizational interests and autonomy among professional associations. We also explicitly examined how these factors impact upon the extent to which ethical ideals serve as the basis for policy decisions by the seven organizations. Our results illuminate how the policy interests of professional associations are influenced in important ways by interorganizational linkages. Over and over again we demonstrate how multiple interorganizational connections link associations' members, leaders, and the organizations themselves to larger and more powerful external organizational entities and centers of interests.

Ethics Versus Interests

As the High Risk case illustrates, linkages tying professional societies to the corporate and nonprofit sectors are clearly influential in shaping the definition of associations' interests on controversial policy issues. The reality of such connections involving structured patterns of overlapping interests, ideological affinities, and resource dependencies raises serious questions concerning the ability of these organizations to act on the basis of disinterested ethical principles as opposed to political considerations related to interorganizational ties. Our findings indicate that these structural relationships produce effects that, depending on their direction and extent, can either facilitate or inhibit the organizational autonomy of professional associations where controversial public policy issues are concerned.

As noted earlier, the relative *absence* of explicit concerns with and commitments to ethical standards regarding the internal policy decisions and related behaviors of professional associations often appeared to contribute to confusion and conflict within these organizations where the High Risk bills were concerned. In some associations, members who were committed to ethical ideals and principles at the individual level (per organizationally endorsed codes of ethics) found that in the case of the High Risk legislation, their association's leadership was unwilling to base internal policy commitments on those same principles at the organizational level. It is clear that, for the most part, professional societies have not adopted ethical standards of conduct that would obligate associations as *organizations* to abide by the same ethical principles that apply in most cases to individual members.

Given the scope and variety of the evidence we presented, the frequent absence of concern among professional associations with ethical standards at the organizational level (especially where controversial policy issues are concerned) is not surprising. It is less a matter of oversight and more a reflection of the reality of important interorganizational linkages and related political considerations. As long as the issue of ethical behavior is restricted to the individual level and the same ethical standards fail to be explicitly applied at the organizational level, this arrangement is likely to continue to confuse and muffle debates regarding potential conflicts of interests within professional societies. At the same time, the continuation of this situation will also permit existing interorganizational relationships and linkages which compromise the potential for organizational autonomy and ethical behavior to go unnoticed, unchallenged, unchecked, and unchanged.

Interests and Autonomy

Total structural autonomy for professional societies which are, for the most part, relatively small and resource-dependent entities, is an unlikely prospect. This means that as long as policy-making boards and organizational units themselves are bound by multiple, potent connections to the interests of external constituencies, especially corporations, the structural basis for autonomy will be severely compromised. As a result, the opportunities and incentives to direct the organizations to act in ways consistent with the ethical ideals applicable to individual members will also be minimized.

In order to maximize the potential for organizational autonomy and ethically guided behavior among professional societies on controversial policy issues, our study indicates the need for these organizations to be structurally independent. Such independence is facilitated by minimal interpenetration levels among association leaders, patterns of organizational revenue sources which minimize the importance of external organizational funding, and by sponsorship patterns which link associations' memberships more to the public than to the private sector. The presence of at least two of these conditions appear to be prerequisites for the degree of organizational autonomy necessary to permit and encourage association policy makers to involve the organizations in public health policy issues according to positions based on ethical principles (at the organizational level) and the best available evidence.

Of course, political factors and political influence (in the sense of overlapping and reciprocal material interests as well as ideological affinities) are not likely to ever be totally excluded from science generally or professional associations specifically. This reality was recognized and expressed by most of the informants in the study. One congressional source expressed a widely shared sentiment in this regard: "We realize that there is no such thing as a lack of politics in the scientific or medical communities." However, despite the persistent reality of internal politics in the medical and scientific communities, our data indicate that the significance, the directness, and the extent of the political influence of private sector organizational interests and power upon the policy decisions of professional associations can be reduced. This would involve shifts in interorganizational linkages that would increase the nature, character, and extent of connections between professional associations and the public sector.

Autonomy and Policy

Our findings related to the connections between organizational ethics, interests, autonomy, and policy increase our ability to understand and explain the structural bases of politically motivated versus ethically informed (and evidence-based) internal policy decisions of professional societies on controversial health policy issues. The data make it clear that we cannot assume that associations of health and safety professionals will act on either the basis of ethical principles or upon the narrow, economic self-interests of the membership. Instead, the evidence indicates that where ethics and interests are concerned, the relative influence of these factors upon organizational policies is strongly affected by the patterns of linkages that exist between the associations and their external organizational environments.

Our results indicate that if professional societies wish to be perceived and evaluated as ethical, autonomous, and credible actors in public policy debates, they must do more than insist upon ethical standards for individual members. They must also attend to the divestment of interorganizational linkages that bind them to external private sector interests and constituencies. At the same time they must also develop and pursue publicly stated ethical principles and standards applicable to the organization as a whole. To the extent that these conditions do not obtain, then professional associations will continue to be vulnerable to charges of conflicting interests and/or hidden agendas--especially where controversial policy issues such as the High Risk legislation are concerned.

Health Professionals and Reform

Instead of focusing upon the political and policy preferences of health professionals as individuals, the results of this research suggest the importance of considering how the role of professionals as a force for change is conditioned by their organizations. As our data indicate, professional societies as potential agents of reform are strongly influenced by interorganizational connections that predispose their policy preferences in either liberal or conservative directions. By taking this approach, we gain a clearer understanding of how structural factors operative at the organizational level influence sympathies among health and safety professionals toward social reforms and the prospects of organized collective action by such individuals through their associations as agents of social change.

While we did not attempt to systematically assess the importance of professional associations to the policy reform-process, several informants (cited throughout the book) commented on this issue. The consistency of their remarks indicates that within the occupational health policy arena, these associations are viewed by the core actor groups and by members of Congress and their staff as significant actors in debates over policy issues. Both sides clearly and openly engaged in efforts aimed at either enlisting their support or at the very least neutralizing their involvement. These actions suggest that the cultural authority of these groups represents an important resource in political struggles related to the development and enactment of occupational health policy reform legislation.

While they are important to the policy process, the High Risk case makes it clear that professional associations are divided as a political force on occupational health policy reforms. Our findings concerning the nature and extent of the linkages between professional societies and the private or public sectors underscore how the politics and policies of these organizations are likely to be influenced more by the effects of interorganizational linkages than by "new class" membership[3] or by individual member's subjective perceptions of "contradictory class locations" (Oppenheimer 1985:92, 145). This means that while these factors *may*, at the individual level, be associated with alienation, frustration, and policy inclinations favoring social change and reform among professionals, their *organizations* are not likely to support policy reforms consistent with these impulses unless the associations are structurally independent from the private sector at both the leadership and organizational levels.

Close and multiple linkages between professional associations and the public sector do not, in and of themselves, guarantee support for progressive policy reforms by these groups. However, as this study has illustrated, interorganizational structural linkages are critical factors influencing their policy decisions. As we have seen, the absence of extensive connections between professional societies and the private sector and/or the presence of such linkages with the public sector establish the structural preconditions which make their support for progressive reform policies much more likely and at much stronger levels than would otherwise be the case.

In the future, professional societies are likely to become increasingly involved in the development of public policy issues.[4] At the same time they are also likely to continue to be targets of the competing core actor organizations in their efforts to mobilize and utilize the cultural authority of professional societies as "scientific experts" in policy matters which relate to their areas of expertise. Even so, despite the likelihood of increased participation by professional societies in the national policy formation process, unless existing patterns of interorganizational linkages are modified, we are likely to see a continuation of the strong tendencies observed in the High Risk case. That is, professional associations, in most instances, will act not as agents of reform, but rather as agents for the status quo.

PROFESSIONS, POLICY, AND THE PROBLEM OF THEORY

As noted in chapter 2, an initial problem we confronted was the absence of an explicit theoretical tradition for framing and addressing questions related to the participation of professional associations in the policy-formation process. Despite this handicap, we demonstrated how it was possible to construct a coherent theoretical approach and useful orienting concepts by combining various themes and ideas from the sociological literature related to both organizations and the professions. Our theoretical orientation represents, we believe, an important step forward in terms of developing conceptual tools for analyzing and assessing the bases of policy participation decisions among professional associations. It is our view that the theoretical approach and the specific orienting concepts applied and refined in this study will find wider applications in other studies addressing the interorganizational and contextual bases of organizational behavior--especially where association policies are concerned.

A particularly important feature of our theoretical approach is that it illustrates how the complex "embeddedness" issue (Granovetter 1985) related to organizations and their environments can be fruitfully addressed and clarified. The core-periphery imagery provides a useful analytical framework which permits a better understanding of how the interests and power of core organizational actors form an important context that conditions the policy preferences of professional associations in the occupational health policy process. Also, by conceptualizing interorganizational linkages in terms of multiple, specific connections involving sponsorship, interpenetration, and resource dependency, our approach contributes to a more complete under-standing of how and why structured patterns of interdependence and power inequalities between core-periphery organizations act to produce predictable association policy outcomes. By framing the policy participation decisions and/or activities of professional societies in these terms, it is possible to more completely address and assess what appear to be important, causal linkages related to the political dimension of organizational policy making.

In addition to the emphasis which our theoretical approach places upon structural linkages, the model also demonstrates how the influence of contextual factors may be addressed. By framing organizational behavior within a political-choice format, the model illustrates how events and circumstances interact with structural linkages to produce either conjunctural or separate effects upon the policy-related decisions of the focal actors. This aspect of our theory addresses the dynamic qualities of organizational environments and policy making. It illustrates that organizations are not only embedded within interorganizational networks via structural linkages, but also that they (i.e., their members and leaders) are exposed to and experience the influence of shifting internal and external environments.

As a result of our experiences in applying the central ideas and concepts of our theoretical approach, we can offer some suggestions on how the model may be modified to make it even more efficacious. For example, future research related to understanding the policy decisions of professional associations would be enhanced by the development of additional theoretical constructs for aiding in the identification of other structural linkages between these groups and core actor organizations (such as, for example, hidden interpenetration). Also, it would be helpful to construct a more explicit and systematic conceptualization of how contextual factors may be integrated into and articulated with the posited, causal linkage factors in influencing the policy outcomes of professional societies.

The conceptual categories related to the policy positions and resource-commitment decisions of professional associations represent another area where refinements could be made. Qualitative and quantitative measures of

these factors could be sharpened to better specify how they may be characterized, measured, tracked over time, and understood as including a dual reality.
That is, as we saw with High Risk legislation, the focal actors may adopt
formal, public policy positions on legislative issues, but at the same time there
may also coexist an informal, unstated policy stance that qualifies in important
ways an organization's publicly stated policy. Also, with regard to resource-
commitment levels we can see a similar practice at work. That is, there may
be both public and concealed resource-commitment levels and patterns. A
theoretical model and/or concepts that address these thorny issues in a more
precise and systematic fashion would be most helpful in further refining the
basic approach and directions taken in this study.

CONCLUDING REMARKS AND OBSERVATIONS

> "Medicine is a social science, and politics nothing but
> medicine on a grand scale."
>   Rudolf Virchow 1848, cited in Taylor and Rieger
>   1984, p. 202.

This project grew out of an interest in exploring and developing a better
understanding of the links between work, health, medicine, politics, and policy.
In this sense, its objectives are directly linked to and framed within the
general orientation and traditions of social medicine as established by Virchow
and others beginning in the mid-1800s. Our results illustrate how the
involvement of health and safety professional societies in the occupational
health policy process is conditioned in important ways by what are essentially
political factors and considerations. Such findings are consistent with the basic
perspective of social medicine which views medicine, politics, and policy as
inextricably woven together into a complex matrix with far-reaching effects for
the health and well-being of workers and all other members of the society.

Health Policy and Corporate Hegemony

An important feature of the political nature of health and health policy to
which our findings relate, but which was not directly addressed by our
research focus or orienting questions, concerns the issue of hegemony. (This
was the subject of the Navarro quote at the beginning of this chapter.) The
relevance of this concept to our topic is illustrated by the extensive influence
of the business community in the health policy process. As we have seen, the
corporate sector has the power and resources that allow it to shape the policy

agenda generally where occupational health issues are concerned. More specifically, it is also able to influence, in important ways, the participation of professional societies in the development of particular legislation such as the High Risk bills. Such patterns of influence support the conclusion that the organizational actors which collectively comprise the corporate sector occupy what could be characterized as a position of structural, political, and cultural hegemony where occupational health policy issues are concerned. This means that the extent to which the activities of professional societies in formulating occupational health legislation favor corporate interests is reflective *not* of a corporate conspiracy to generate such outcomes, but rather as a consequence of the existence of a hegemonic corporate culture.[5]

This study did not directly address the issue of corporate hegemony within health, medical, and safety professional organizations. However, our focus upon the structural linkages connecting the interests and power of the business community to professional societies did touch upon some of the mechanisms through which corporate dominance is channeled in the spheres of science, medicine, and policy. In this sense our findings illuminate important aspects of corporate hegemony by illustrating the role played by structural and political linkages in the creation of policy preferences and ideological affinities among health and safety professional groups for the views and interests of the business community.

Future research related to corporate hegemony within the health policy process should be aimed at exploring the nature and extent of other indirect forms of corporate domination over professional associations. This could be accomplished by examining both the macro- and micro-level structures and processes involved in the creation, dissemination, and acceptance of a corporate *weltanschuuang*[6] where occupational health policy issues are concerned. Such efforts might include, for example, inquiries into the processes of selective recruitment and socialization of the personnel who are drawn into the occupational health and safety professions at both the rank-and-file level as well as at the leadership levels of the professional societies in these areas. This kind of research could add an important dimension to our understanding of how corporate organizational structures create, maintain, and transmit hegemonic organizational cultures and how they shape the political and ideological affinities of health, medical, and safety professionals.

The Future of Risk Notification

At a more immediate and practical level, the defeat of the High Risk legislation in 1988 did not signal the end of the political consideration of, or debate over, risk notification as a policy issue. As noted earlier, the High Risk bills were reintroduced in the 101st Congress (1989-1990), but due to the conflicts over S.79 and the absence of any new political compromises, they languished in the subcommittees. In the 102nd Congress (1991-1992) risk notification was abandoned as a separate legislative initiative by organized labor; instead, it was included as only one provision of a much more comprehensive effort to reform the original OSH Act (*Congressional Record* 1991a:E2858-60; 1991b:S11833-45; Kwik 1991:16). Meanwhile, the DOE and NIOSH notification projects continue to move forward and add legitimacy to the idea that the federal government has a responsibility to notify workers whose workplace exposures increase their risks for developing occupational diseases (*OSH Reporter* 1988; U.S. Congress: House 1989). Taken together, these developments mean that the professional associations profiled in this study will continue to be confronted with the question of how to address risk notification both as a national legislative agenda item and at subnational policy levels in forums such as within plants, union-negotiated agreements, and federal agencies.

Given the extent of corporate hegemony within the occupational health and safety policy domain, it is ironic that even the health and safety professional associations most closely linked to the private sector helped contribute to the elevation of risk notification to the high levels of attention and concern it has received as a public policy issue. Partly as a result of the success that all professional associations have experienced in getting more public and corporate resources devoted to enhancing the expertise of their members, the technical competence of health and safety specialists has improved.[7] This situation has enhanced the abilities of these professionals to detect the presence of toxic and/or hazardous substances in the workplace and also aided in the identification of the negative health effects of exposures to such substances. Through efforts aimed at improving the technical skills of their members, the professional societies collectively have produced an increasingly sophisticated, technically supported, and difficult to deny "body count" of worker casualties due to an ever-increasing array of hazardous workplace substances. This is important because the development of policy reforms in occupational health and safety has historically been tied to undeniable body counts. As one corporate health and safety director put it:

> In the past . . . it's been the body counts that have led us to what our problems are. And if the name of the game is to protect employees and the liabilities of the larger corporation, one must move toward prevention and early detection to minimize those liabilities (cited in Walsh 1987:131).

The debates over the merits of and need for the High Risk legislation frequently centered around the idea of uncertainties. They involved unknowns related to the likely consequences of the legislation for businesses and the extent to which the currently available evidence was compelling enough to justify the enactment of the bills. Our results indicate that those professional associations with extensive structural linkages closely tying their members and leaders to the public sector favored a risk notification policy which, to the extent that the evidence was uncertain, erred on the side of caution. That meant favoring the protection of workers' health through support for enacting the High Risk legislation. By contrast, faced with the uncertainties of the available evidence, the leaders of professional associations closely linked by structural ties to the private sector appeared to require a higher standard of evidence. From their perspective, the evidence was not sufficient to justify lending their associations' support to the High Risk legislation. However, because of the structural linkages between these organizations and private sector employers, our results indicate that their evaluation of the evidence was influenced by the potential costs and consequences for the corporate organizations that they were linked to in a kind of patron-to-sycophant relationship. In short, the policy-making leadership of these organizations demanded "more bodies."

As has so often been the case in the past, the workers were caught between the conflicting demands among both professionals and politicians for more "scientific evidence" which would be sufficient to justify the High Risk program. In order to satisfy both friendly and hostile demands for evidence supporting the need for the legislation, workers would first have to be made ill or die to provide it. In fact, the High Risk bill reintroduced in 1989 by Congressman Gaydos (H.R. 3067) "prohibits the Risk Assessment Board from considering animal studies and, instead permits only the use of human studies" (*Congressional Record* 1989a:H4697). This provision alone ensures that more workers would have to become ill or die from exposures to hazardous and/or toxic substances in the workplace in order to provide the basis for any future risk notification program.

In spite of the defeat of S.79 in 1988, inaction on the High Risk bills in the 101st Congress, and the political struggles attendant to the effort at reforming the OSH Act in the 102nd Congress, it is likely that risk notification will eventually be elevated to the status of national public policy. However, as our study suggests, it is also likely that its enactment will first be preceded by various kinds of agency-level risk notification programs as well as the accumulation of additional studies documenting the negative health effects of workplace toxins in producing higher and ever more undeniable worker body counts.

In the absence of political compromises involving substantial corporate concessions, or perhaps a major, well-publicized workplace crisis, or a substantial alteration of the political context, risk notification will persist as an unresolved public health issue. This means that we will continue to read stories such as this: "Although the company and the state [of North Carolina] have known since 1989 [that] . . . the [work] site [was] highly contaminated with numerous hazardous chemicals . . . there has been no worker screening . . . and no clean-up" (LeRoy 1991). At the same time, it is also likely that the health and safety professional associations profiled in this study will continue to participate in the legislative development of this issue through the adoption of policies that reflect the potent influence of interorganizational linkages. These ties will continue to bind association policies--to a greater or lesser extent--to the interests and power of external organizational constituencies which have predictable interests and preferences where policy outcomes related to risk notification are concerned.

ACRONYMS

AAOHN	American Association of Occupational Health Nurses
AAOM	American Academy of Occupational Medicine
AARP	American Association of Retired Persons
ACGIH	American Conference of Governmental Industrial Hygienists
ACOM	American College of Occupational Medicine
ACS	American Cancer Society
AEA	American Electronics Association
AFL-CIO	American Federation of Labor-Congress of Industrial Organizations
AFSCME	American Federation of State, County, and Municipal Employees
AIA	American Insurance Association
AIDS	Acquired Immune Deficiency Syndrome
AIHA	American Industrial Hygiene Association
ALA	American Lung Association
AMA	American Medical Association
AMC	American Mining Congress
AMPAC	American Medical Political Action Committee
AOMA	American Occupational Medical Association
APA	American Psychological Association
APHA	American Public Health Association
API	American Petroleum Institute
ARCO	Atlantic Richfield Corporation
ASAE	American Society of Association Executives
ASSE	American Society of Safety Engineers
AT&T	American Telephone and Telegraph Corporation
BLS	Bureau of Labor Statistics
CDC	Centers for Disease Control
CMA	Chemical Manufacturers Association
DHHS	Department of Health and Human Services
DOE	Department of Energy

FAA	Federal Aviation Administration
FACOSH	Federal Advisory Council on Occupational Safety and Health
FEC	Federal Election Commission
GE	General Electric Corporation
HCS	Hazard Communication Standard
HRG	Public Citizen Health Research Group
IBM	International Business Machines Corporation
IRC	Internal Revenue Code
IRS	Internal Revenue Service
IUD	Industrial Union Department (of the AFL-CIO)
MSDS	Material Safety Data Sheets
NACOSH	National Advisory Council on Occupational Safety and Health
NAM	National Association of Manufacturers
NCI	National Cancer Institute
NIOSH	National Institute for Occupational Safety and Health
NPCA	National Paint and Coatings Association
OSH Act	Occupational Safety and Health Act of 1970
OSHA	Occupational Safety and Health Administration
OSHRC	Occupational Safety and Health Review Commission
OTA	Office of Technology Assessment
PACs	Political Action Committees
PATCO	Professional Air Traffic Controllers Organization
SEIU	Service Employees International Union
TLVs	Threshold Limit Values
UAW	United Auto Workers
UMW	United Mine Workers
USWA	United Steel Workers of America
WISH	Workers Institute for Safety and Health

NOTES

CHAPTER ONE

1. Public Law 91-596, Section 5a(1).

2. The OSH Act created several government agencies to carry out the main functions of the statute including: (1) The Occupational Safety and Health Administration (OSHA); (2) The National Institute for Occupational Safety and Health (NIOSH); (3) The Occupational Safety and Health Review Commission (OSHRC); (4) advisory committees: The National Advisory Committee on Occupational Safety and Health (NACOSH) and The Federal Advisory Council on Occupational Safety and Health (FACOSH). The task of conducting surveys and collecting injury and illness data was assigned to the Bureau of Labor Statistics (BLS). For a summary of the functions of the various agencies see Nothstein (1981).

3. Laumann and Knoke (1987) use the concept of consequential actors to denote organizations with interests related to various national policy issues and who have power to shape policies relevant to their interests.

4. Peak associations are organizations created to represent the collective interests of several organizations with similar views and objectives. They are typically enduring, incorporated entities rather than transitory, loose coalitions. Several authors have utilized this concept (e.g., Domhoff 1978, 1983; Wallace and Rubin 1986).

5. The concept of cultural authority was developed by Starr (1982). It refers to the idea that health professionals (especially physicians) possess specialized knowledge that is widely accepted in the culture as legitimate and which requires that their judgments in their area of expertise be taken as definitive. As Starr says, "cultural authority entails the construction of reality through definitions of fact and value" (1982:13).

6. This conclusion is based on both interview sources and information provided in the Congressional Research Service publications, *Major Legislation of the Congress* and *The Congressional Quarterly Almanac* for the 1968-88 period.

7. Liberal reform generally refers to utilizing government policies as vehicles for redressing patterns of gross inequalities among various social groups. The concept is virtually synonymous with "social policy" in the sense that this term refers to policies designed to reduce social inequalities. See Noble (1986:237-243) for a discussion of these issues.

8. Ratcliffe and Wallack (1985-86:217) define these concepts as follows: *Primary Prevention* is "the removal of the root cause of the disease through such interventions as immunization, modification of personal behavior, and/or reduction or elimination of adverse environmental factors." *Secondary Prevention* is "the detection, diagnosis, and containment of disease, usually through screening procedures." *Tertiary Prevention* is "the amelioration, treatment, or cure of clinical disease."

9. Health promotion and protection are discussed in Ratcliffe et al. (1984) and Ratcliffe and Wallack (1985-86). The former term refers to the view that many diseases in modern societies are caused by and reflective of personal decisions regarding one's habits and lifestyle. The latter concept views the causes of many diseases as grounded in social structural factors such as the unequal distribution of economic resources, occupational stress, and environmental pollution.

10. This characterization of health policy requires important qualifications. The advent of the fiscal crisis of the state has caused an increasing recognition that health policy, even if narrowly limited to government organization and financing of some types of health services, is now increasingly linked to resource choices and allocations that are shifting health policy issues into the redistributive policy arena. The problems and limits of state intervention in health policy are discussed by Renaud (1975) and Navarro (1982). More specifically, the growing problems of state financing of health services and how this may be viewed as involving the ideas of rationing and redistribution are considered in de Kervasdoue and Rodwin (1984).

11. Public policies may also produce results whereby employment-related health problems are paid for via general tax revenue funded programs (e.g., Sheehan 1982:69; U.S. Congress: Office of Technology Assessment 1985:307; Knudsen 1987:2514).

12. In this context, ideology refers to "the ethical, juridical, political, esthetical, and philosophical ideas about social reality as well as the set of customs, practices and behaviors which consciously or unconsciously reflect that vision of reality" (Navarro 1980:192).

13. According to this perspective, highly educated professionals are members of a "new class" and "find their source of power not in money or property but in expertise" (Hargrove 1986:8). In general, new class theory asserts that professionals are likely to hold liberal political views which favor an "interventionist agenda of government into business, . . . and a reformist

approach to political issues in general" (Hunter 1980:156). While a number of studies have addressed the issue of "liberalism" among professionals (e.g., Brint 1984, 1987; Ehrenreich and Ehrenreich 1977; Gouldner 1979; Lamont 1987; Macy 1988; McAdams 1987; Oppenheimer 1985), they have focused largely upon the origins and distribution of liberal versus conservative attitudes among "new class" members and the results been mixed. This study illustrates how the discourse aimed at refining new class theory may be usefully informed by the inclusion of an interorganizational perspective. Our focus upon the involvement of professional associations in policy reform struggles moves us beyond the study of attitudes (at an individual level of analysis) and provides insights into how interorganizational linkages influence the policy preferences, interests, and activities of professionals--as organized groups--on social reform issues.

14. The idea that professionals may occupy contradictory class locations refers to the reality that many professionals today are employed by large organizations where they are semiautonomous employees.

CHAPTER TWO

1. This line is from the 1976 movie *All The President's Men* (Warner Bros. Inc.); the screenplay was based on the book (same title) by Carl Bernstein and Bob Woodward (1974).

2. The issues of interests and power are especially important to the theoretical orientation in this study. For a discussion of how business and worker interests are related to political issues see Balbus (1971). The ability of business or labor to protect and/or extend their economic and/or political interests in the area of occupational health and safety policy issues is directly related to the relative power of the two groups. For a discussion of the issue of working-class power, political issues, and social-welfare programs see Esping-Andersen (1985).

3. By conceptualizing organizations in terms of "masters," we avoid the problem of reifying such entities to the point where "they" (the organizations) are viewed as having "needs" or "goals" apart from internal, policy-making "masters". For a discussion of this issue see Zey-Ferrell and Aiken (1981).

4. Decisions regarding sponsorship subtypes for each organization were based upon interviews with association staff members as well as organizational publications. By combining data from these sources, we were able to develop consistent estimates of sector employment patterns and percentages for each association's membership during the 1985-88 period.

5. To apply the interpenetration subtypes, it was necessary to resolve three issues: (1) the definition of administrative and executive positions, (2) the

identification of the individuals who served on association policy-setting boards during 1985-88, and (3) the computation of the extent of interpenetration. Administrative and executive positions in for-profit firms were defined as those above the rank of first line supervisors or coordinators (i.e., general supervisors, department and region managers/directors, and executives such as corporate vice presidents). The logic for this classification scheme was based partly upon interview data concerning the occupational duties and responsibilities of board members employed by for-profit firms and also on the basis of the literature related to occupational locations and types (e.g., Hall 1986; Rothman 1987; Ford 1988). The individuals who served as association officers and board members during 1985-88 were identified along with their employment locations and job titles for the year 1987 (as a midpoint in the period). The extent of interpenetration was calculated by dividing the number of officers and board members who held executive and/or administrative positions in for-profit firms by the total number of officers and board members in each association (the percentages ranged from 0 percent to 95 percent).

6. To apply the resource dependency subtypes it was necessary to clarify each association's revenue sources. This was accomplished via a series of steps beginning with a determination of the extent to which the associations' annual budgets were financially dependent upon membership dues versus other income sources. Each association's federal form 990 tax return served as the primary means for making this determination. (These documents are a matter of public record.) The extent of each association's financial dependence upon membership dues was calculated by dividing the annual revenues received from dues by the total annual revenue for 1987 (as a midpoint of the 1985-88 period).

7. The resource-commitment continuum designations are defined as follows: (1) and (3) at both ends of the continuum refer to varying levels of resources allocated by the associations in support of their basic policy decisions in terms of three resource-commitment levels and types, depending upon the extent and vigor of support for or opposition to the legislation (i.e., from strong support: three "pluses" [+ + +], to strong opposition: three "minuses" [- - -]). Neutrality (2) indicates both a formal, neutral basic policy position on the reform legislation and the absence of any evidence related to the commitment of organizational resources either for or against the legislation.

CHAPTER THREE

1. Schulte and Ringen (1984:485) cite several examples of federal statutes which were passed in the 1970s and which helped to change attitudes and ideas related to risk notification: The OSH Act (1970), the Mine Safety and Health Act of 1977, the Toxic Substances Control Act (1976), and the Health Services Research, Health Statistics, and Health Care Technology Act of 1978.

2. These demonstration projects were located in Tyler, Texas (asbestos exposure), and Louisville, Kentucky (vinyl chloride exposure) (U.S. Congress: Senate, 1977:85).

3. The congressional oversight hearings on OSHA in 1974 and 1976 looked into the health effects of workplace exposures to various toxic substances including asbestos, vinyl chloride, lead, and kepone (U.S. Congress: House, 1974:190-197; 235-244; Mintz 1984:411-414).

4. This outcome was ironic in that PATCO had supported Reagan in the 1980 presidential campaign. The organization expected him to be sympathetic to their concerns over working conditions and wages (Tesh 1988:108-111).

5. The Hazard Communication Standard (HCS) took effect in November 1985 and May 1986. The Senate Committee on Labor and Human Relations Report summarized the effects of the standard and its shortcomings insofar as notification was concerned. In general, the HCS required only that material safety data sheets (MSDS) be attached to hazardous materials used in manufacturing. The MSDS provide information on the negative health effects of the chemicals but do not provide any specific information about increased risks for developing occupational diseases for workers as a result of his or her past exposures to toxic substances. (U.S. Congress: Senate 1987b:17-19).

CHAPTER FOUR

1. The 30 percent notification trigger was suggested by Dr. Irving Selikoff, an internationally known clinician and researcher in occupational diseases. He is now professor emeritus, Mount Sinai School of Medicine of the City University of New York (U.S. Congress: House, 1987a:249; *Congressional Record* 1986:H9421-9422).

2. In a related development, the Senate Committee on Small Business, chaired by Senator Dale Bumpers (D-Ark.) held hearings in June 1987, on the impact of S.79 on small businesses. During these hearings, Senator Metzenbaum inserted twenty nine letters from corporate and trade associations

which were then publicly supporting the legislation (U.S. Congress: Senate, 1987c:21-49).

3. The House Subcommittee on Health and Safety and the Senate Subcommittee on Labor maintain informal files of documents related to the High Risk legislation. References to these records in the book are indicated according to the House or Senate and the time periods when the legislation was actively being considered by Congress (i.e., U.S. Congress: House, 1985-88; U.S. Congress: Senate, 1986-88). Access to these records is granted on an informal basis through contacts with the subcommittee staff members.

4. The importance of the liability-restricting, precedent-setting provisions incorporated into the revised High Risk bills anticipated the expansion of worker concerns with occupational health issues in the 1990s. This issue was addressed in a speech at a conference on occupational safety, health, and industrial hygiene:

> According to David Hayes, an attorney with the Washington, D.C., firm of Hogan & Hartson. "The 1990s are going to be a very busy time on the occupational health and safety side."
> . . . He predicted that [in the 1990s] job safety and health finally will get the kind of attention . . . that environmental concerns enjoyed in the 1970s and 1980s (*OSH Reporter* 1989:755).

5. The involvement of the Crum & Forster Insurance company with the High Risk bills makes for an interesting "minicase study" illustrating how interlocks within the corporate community influenced its position on the legislation.   Since 1983, the company has been a subsidiary of Xerox Corporation (*Wall Street Journal* 1988a:31). In the 1980s Xerox was involved in a long and expensive court case in New York state related to toxic waste and ground water contamination (*Wall Street Journal* 1988b:48). The court case was resolved by a confidential but expensive settlement (*Wall Street Journal* 1989:B5; Weiser 1989:1 & A8). As a result of that case, Xerox management reportedly put pressure on Crum & Forster to drop its support for the High Risk bills. As a senior congressional staffer put it: "Xerox is in the middle of a vigorous legal challenge over some environmental exposures so they have taken Crum and Forster off of the [High Risk] legislation."

6. Evidence of the continuing concern of the chemical industry with its image can be found in *Chemicalweek* (Coombes 1989:14). The article suggests the need for better public relations to defuse growing popular concerns over the effects of the industry on the environment and to head off potentially restrictive regulatory legislation.

7. The reasons given by informants concerning why some segments of the corporate community supported the legislation included views other than the three themes cited. In general they were more speculative, less subject to confirmation, and centered around three ideas: (1) Some informants suggested that some businesses were supportive because their corporate officers had close ties with Senator Metzenbaum and he was largely responsible for negotiating the revisions in the legislation and lining up most of the business support. (2) A second reason involved the idea that supportive corporations hoped to gain a competitive advantage if the bills passed. Because these companies had most of their production facilities overseas, they would not be affected by the notification costs. (3) The third explanation centered around the reasons for trade association support and was based upon a staff-board distinction. The logic of this approach was explained by a senior Senate staffer opposed to the legislation:

> A lot of the trade associations have staff who are sympathetic to this kind of thing. The problem they have is that they hire Democratic staff members to get access to Democratic members [of Congress], but those staff members, because of their sympathies with the positions of the Democrats do not necessarily get them adequate pictures of what the legislation entails. . . . So you had a situation where very early, some of the staff sort of jerked around their membership and then after the membership found out what they had signed on to, they were livid.

8. The list of individual coalition members was maintained by NAM (National Association of Manufacturers ca., 1988, "Coalition on Disease Notification Membership List"). The list was made public during the Senate debates on S.79 (*Congressional Record* 1988a:S2783-S2784).

9. Federal Election Commission (FEC) records tend to support the view that Senator Hatch was acting at least in part out of concern for his political supporters. According to FEC documents regarding 1987-88 PAC contributions to Senator Hatch's 1988 reelection campaign, approximately $3.8 million was received by the Senator. Much of the money came from corporations and trade associations opposed to the legislative agenda of organized labor-- including the High Risk Act (Federal Election Commission 1987-88 Candidate Index of Supporting Documents (E) Hatch, Orrin G.). Obviously, political contributions are seldom based on single issues and politicians' careers and actions are not built around one bill, but the PAC contribution record is indicative of the extensive corporate tilt underlying the senator's campaign

receipts and suggests a receptiveness to those interests and a willingness to work on their behalf.

10. Interpretations of Senator Bumpers' motives for helping to kill S.79 varied among interview sources. His political friends emphasized his thoughtful reading of the bill's merits as leading to his opposition of it. Less sanguine sources cited corporate influence, especially that of small business, as the basis for his position. These conflicting accounts make it difficult to know for certain why Senator Bumpers acted as he did. However, FEC records provide some support for the influence of small business theory. During the 1985-86 election cycle, Senator Bumpers received over $1.7 million in PAC contributions. Much of the money came from literally dozens (if not hundreds) of contributions from small businesses and small business trade associations that were opposed to S.79 (Federal Election Commission 1985-86 Candidate Index of Supporting Documents (E), Bumpers, Dale.).

11. Although S.79 died, the High Risk legislation was reintroduced in the 101st Congress (*Congressional Record* 1989a:H4696-98; 1989b:S2570; 1989c:S2673-80; 1989d:H4844). However, in both Houses the bills remained dormant and the 101st Congress ended without any action taken to move the bills forward. Despite the failure of the legislative effort, both NIOSH and the Department of Energy (DOE) are moving ahead with risk notification projects on their own initiatives. The DOE project involves notifying workers who may have been exposed to beryllium dust which can produce "disabling and even deadly [effects]" (*OSH Reporter* 1988:501). The NIOSH notification project was summarized by the agency's director, Dr. J. Donald Millar during congressional oversight hearings in 1989:

> NIOSH has completed a preliminary assessment of 132 NIOSH studies initially identified as potentially warranting notification and have narrowed this group to 34 studies. NIOSH has evaluated five of these and will initiate individual notification for two cohorts in 1989. Of the remaining studies, a NIOSH contractor is presently evaluating 25 studies, using the guidelines from our Board of Scientific Counselors and the NIOSH-prepared prototype evaluations. These evaluations will be completed before 1991. The remaining four studies will be evaluated in 1991. NIOSH policy for all ongoing and future research is to conduct individual notification as an integral part of all epidemiologic research we support (U.S. Congress: House, 1989:23).

In the 102nd Congress the basic features of the High Risk legislation were folded into a more extensive legislative effort supported by the AFL-CIO known as the "Comprehensive Occupational Safety and Health Reform Act." The legislation was introduced in both the House and Senate on August 1, 1991, as H.R. 3160 and S.1622 (*Congressional Record* 1991a:E2858-60; 1991b:S11833-45).

CHAPTER FIVE

1. Sources: 1987 Form 990 federal tax returns for the AMA, ACGIH, AAOHN, AIHA, AOMA, ASSE; 1986 return for the APHA.

2. The IRS Form 990 federal tax return for nonprofit groups requires that tax-exempt organizations list revenues according to general categories such as membership dues, interest, dividends, program service revenue, and "other". Since finer-grained information on association income sources is not required on the 990 forms, it is difficult to directly trace interorganizational financial linkages. However, by piecing together information from the 990 forms and other sources, it is possible to develop a relatively clear picture of such linkages.

3. Incorporation under state laws as a nonprofit organization does not automatically guarantee federal tax-exempt status; such organizations must also meet criteria established by the IRS (Jacobs 1986:370).

4. In addition to tracking policy developments, on some issues the organizations may be proactive in the sense of initiating policies of interest to the associations' members. This is likely to involve the utilization of contacts with sympathetic legislators who will introduce legislation that an association's leadership and/or membership wish to see passed. The AMA's long-standing effort at malpractice insurance reform is an illustration of this process (e.g., U.S. Congress: Senate, 1986).

5. This generic policy-making process description is a summary of procedures described by association staffers in interviews and as outlined in association bylaws.

6. Informants reported that although board members' preferences largely determine association policies, they also indicated that the board members are cautious and seldom take positions that they think might offend the membership base. As one informant stated: "There's just as much politics in professional societies as anyplace else, and board members can't risk getting too far from the membership [on policy matters]."

7. These included association documents, publications, and interviews with association staff members, congressional staff with association leadership contacts, association members, and other sources with connections among leaders of the seven associations.

8. The calculation of the AMA sponsorship pattern involved combining data from two sources (Roback et al. 1987; Marder et al. 1988). The data indicate that in 1986 there were 569,160 physicians in the United States. Of that total, approximately 496,000 were either self-employed (full or part owners of their own practices) or employed by private entities.

The calculation of interpenetration for AMA officers and/or directors presents some problems in that many of them are executive-administrators within their own incorporated practices. At the same time, many also occupy positions on boards of directors of various corporations (e.g., insurance, investment companies, and banks). Taking these factors into consideration, it is possible to develop an alternative definition of this factor which produces an interpenetration level of 68 percent for AMA officers and/or directors.

9. The corporate sponsorship percentage for the AOMA includes physicians employed by private corporations as well as those in private practices.

CHAPTER SIX

1. As a result of a "massive letter writing campaign to Congress" and personal contacts involving AAOHN senior staff members and members of Congress, OSHA's final rule was changed in accordance with the interests and concerns of the organization. (Sources: Personal interviews and the *AAOHN Journal* 1987a:131).

2. We must be cautious in ascribing autonomy to professional associations. In the case of the AAOHN, even though membership dues account for 70 percent of its annual revenues, at least *some* of those dues are paid by corporate employers. The exact amount and percentage could not be determined by the available data.

3. In many respects, the AAOHN effort can be viewed as part of an even larger "professionalization project" involving the entire nursing profession (cf. Brannon 1990:516).

4. Any move in the direction of parity with other occupational health and safety-related professions would be likely to have a positive impact upon average salaries of occupational health nurses, which have traditionally ranked below those of other professionals in this area. For example, in the mid-1980s the average salary range for nurses working in industry was $18,000 to $28,000, "with the highest salaries in the $29,000 to $34,000 bracket" (Wright 1988:551). By contrast, the average net income of physicians in 1985 was $113,200 (*American Medical News* 1987a:17). While the income levels of occupational physicians are difficult to know exactly, they appear to be close to the overall average. In 1988 a corporate recruiter for positions starting at $100,000 noted

that "the outlook for physician-executives is good" (*American Medical News* 1988b:14). Among safety engineers, the 1988 average income was between $45,500 and $47,800 (*Professional Safety* 1989a:29). These comparisons, while inexact, provide some idea of the relative position of nurses' incomes as compared with those of other professionals within the occupational health and safety specialties.

5. This was the only instance of information utilized in the narrative that could not be directly confirmed. However, because of related corroborating evidence it was decided to include it as an illustration of the kinds of pressures the associations experienced as the High Risk legislation was being considered in the Congress.

6. These officials were: Vice President Sharon L. Muckenfuss, Medical Department Manager, Gilbarco, Inc. (owned by General Electric); Secretary Janet L. Good, coordinator, Health Services, Atlantic Richfield; Director Grace O. Rome, Nurse Specialist, IBM (*AAOHN Journal* 1987b: Directory Page).

7. The AAOHN code of ethics is presented in the *AAOHN Journal* (1986:365).

8. This policy was consistent with a long-standing commitment by the association to the protection of workers' health and the "right to know" principle (e.g., APHA Policy Statement No. 8329(PP): "Compensation for and Prevention of Occupational Disease," 1983; also APHA Policy Statement 8416(PP): "Increasing Worker and Community Awareness of Toxic Hazardous in the Workplace," 1985; (both cited in the *American Journal of Public Health* 1985:305).

9. The sympathy of Dr. Robbins to union concerns related to occupational health and safety was underscored by how he was treated by the incoming Reagan administration in 1981: "Dr. Anthony Robbins, the courageous and much admired head of NIOSH in the Carter administration, was given one hour to leave his office by the Reagan people" (Elling 1986:398).

10. These figures were calculated on the basis of Federal Election Commission records for the 1987-88 election cycle (1987-88 Independent Expenditures and Communications Costs. AMPAC; 1988-89 AMPAC Itemized Disbursements January through December).

11. For example, among the 1987-88 AMA officers and trustees, the president elect, Dr. James E. Davis, was the past president of the Chamber of Commerce in Durham, N.C.; he was also a trustee of Blue Cross and Blue Shield, N.C. (*American Medical News* 1987c:17; 1988c:20). Trustee Dr. Ray Gifford served as a Republican member of the Rochester, N.Y., City Council and as a precinct committeeman; he was also a board member of the Ohio Medical PAC (*American Medical News* 1987b:37). Vice Speaker, House of Delegates, Dr. Donald H. Johnson, was a board member and treasurer for the

Louisiana Medical PAC and also a board member of the Louisiana Medical Mutual Insurance Co. where he was active in loss prevention (*American Medical News* 1988d:32). The list goes on and on.

12. AMA officers and trustees known to serve on Blue Cross and Blue Shield Boards include (1987-88) President-Elect Dr. James E. Davis and Trustee Dr. Robert E. McAfee (Sources: *American Medical News* 1987b:37; 1987c:17).

13. "The Hippocratic Oath is the foundation of contemporary medical morality and ethics" (Cockerham 1986:4). (The oath dates to approximately 400 B.C.)

14. In general, TLVs are guidelines established by the ACGIH for safe workplace levels of various toxic substances. The presence of such substances in the work environment below TLVs are not supposed to present elevated risks for disease to workers so exposed. TLVs are not legal standards but many have served as the basis for OSHA standards. See Castleman and Ziem (1988) for a discussion of this topic.

15. The neutrality of ACGIH information has been challenged by Castleman and Ziem (1988). Their controversial article raised the possibility of corporate influence in establishing TLVs and provoked over twenty three commentaries (most of which favored the authors' views) in several issues of volumes fourteen and fifteen of the *American Journal of Industrial Medicine* (1988-1989).

CHAPTER SEVEN

1. This list includes President William T. Nebraska, vice president--Loss Control, Hartford Insurance Group and board members Martin A. Marino, vice president, Johnson and Higgins; James A. Broderick, vice president, Alexander & Alexander; Norman E. LaMontagne, vice president, Johnson and Higgins; Richard E. Botts, vice president, Fred S. James & Co. (*Professional Safety* 1987a:12).

2. The ASSE provides an interesting illustration of interorganizational resource ties in addition to those examined via our model's three structural linkages. For example, the organization's mortgage payments for its recently acquired (1985) headquarters building in Des Plaines, Illinois, were supplemented in 1987 by cash donations from corporations of $20,000. Also, Amoco Corporation (which opposed the High Risk legislation) donated $39,000 worth of equipment to the ASSE headquarters in 1987 (*Professional Safety* 1987b:1).

3. The AOMA officers and board members are especially well connected to the upper levels of the corporate sector. Of the twenty four officers and board members serving in 1987, eleven were medical directors of large

corporations (*Journal of Occupational Medicine* 1987:991 and various other issues). Like ASSE, AOMA also has numerous interorganizational resource linkages to the private sector in addition to those examined via the three structural linkages of our model. For example, in 1983-84 AOMA created a scholarship fund to provide support for would-be physicians to train in occupational medicine. A separate (but affiliated) 501(c)(3) organization was established in 1985 "to fund between 60 and 100 scholarships in occupational medicine over the next ten years" (*Journal of Occupational Medicine* 1985:923). The $5 million needed to support this project was to be raised by a "Campaign Executive Committee. . . [chaired by] James E. Olson, chairman and chief executive officer of the AT&T Company" (Cannella 1987:152). (AT&T opposed the High Risk legislation in Congress.) The AOMA chairman of the scholarship fund noted that:

> Because the vast majority of physicians in occupational medicine are employed by or consult for private industry, the campaign will seek funds from the business organizations that will benefit from . . . these specialists. . . . Approximately 250 to 300 corporations will be solicited over the next year and a half (Cannella 1987:152).

According to the Scholarship Fund's 1986 Form 990 tax return, the organization received a total of $213,950 in corporate grants during the 1982-85 period to study the feasibility of the project. It is interesting to note that virtually all of this initial grant funding ($211,550) was received from companies that were opposed to the High Risk legislation: Exxon, AT&T, Ford, and Mobile.

4. This 88 percent figure was computed on the basis of 440 corporate organizational members out of a total of 499 organizational members as of December 1987, as reported in the *American Industrial Hygiene Association Journal* (1988:A-112-A-117).

CHAPTER EIGHT

1. As an illustration of this point, an article based on this research was submitted to a major sociological journal. Despite praising the merits of the methodology, one anonymous reviewer still complained that "the shock value of the findings are (sic) not very high." By contrast, in a letter responding to a similar type of article exposing corporate influence on Threshold Limit Values (Castleman and Ziem 1988), a veteran industrial hygienist wrote: "After reading the . . . report that disclosed the massive influence U.S. industry holds

over the ACGIH list, I must admit to being shocked" (Ahlberg 1989:233). This contrast illustrates that individual responses to reports of this sort are highly varied. What is yawningly obvious to one person may be shocking and outrageous to another.

2. Social medicine is perhaps best understood as a broad intellectual perspective emphasizing the social origins of health and disease. In its conservative forms it resembles traditional ideas of public health with emphases upon public sanitation, immunization, and engineering. In its more radical forms it represents a view and vision of health and disease which calls for a radical redistribution of power and wealth as the primary means for achieving health through equality. As Navarro (1985:526-527) has noted:

> From the very beginning there have been two major concep-
> tions of health, disease and medicine under capitalism: . . .
> the social and the materialist *and* the clinical and the
> individualist. The first approach represented by Virchow and
> Engels, defined the social causes and origins of health and
> disease, relating them to the power relations in society. . . .
> [Engels] specifically related disease to the social relations of
> production and the class structure that they determined . . .
> This Marxist tradition was introduced in the U.S. in the
> 1930s by Henry Sigerist . . . who had an enormous influence
> on the development of social medicine and public health, not
> only in the U.S. but in other countries as well.

Besides Sigerist, George Rosen was also extremely influential in the develop-
ment of social medicine in the United States. Both held M.D.s and Rosen also earned a Ph.D. in sociology. Their lives and careers overlapped and each influenced the other. Both are now deceased. For overviews of their careers see the special memorial issues of the *Journal of the History of Medicine and Allied Sciences* (Sigerist: April 1958, Vol.XII [No.2], Fulton, ed.; Rosen: July 1978, Vol. XXXIII [No.3], Wilson, ed.).

3. As this study of the High Risk case illustrates, where redistributive reform issues are concerned, professional association policy choices do not appear to reflect the emergence of separate, collective, and cohesive "new class" interests and policies. Instead, at least at the organizational level, professional association policies tend to mirror segmented attitudes, ideological affinities, and interests which are in many ways consonant with more traditional notions of class divisions between workers and business elites.

4. Our findings indicate that professional associations are becoming increasingly involved in political activities and lobbying efforts. As noted earlier, five of the seven organizations either now have or are considering the

establishment of a formal political presence in Washington, D.C. At the same time that professional societies are gearing up for increased political action, there are indications that the federal government is taking an increased interest in the political activities of these and related nonprofit organizations. In 1987 a pair of congressional hearings were held which increased the visibility of all tax-exempt, nonprofit organizations, including professional associations (U.S. Congress, House 1987b; 1987c). The hearings pointed out the relative lack of reliable information on the nonprofit sector: "Remarkably, there are no precise figures on the numbers of nonprofit organizations nationwide. The IRS estimates over 800,000 organizations, double its estimate of 25 years ago. [The American Society of Association Executives estimates that] 501(c)(3) groups . . . [comprise] 43 percent of all tax-exempt organizations. Sections 501(c)(5) and (c)(6) groups make up another 15 percent of the community" (U.S. Congress: House, 1987c:1640). The hearings also highlighted the economic significance of nonprofits where "current operating expenditures of nonprofit organizations totaled $239 billion in 1985, or six percent of GNP" (U.S. Congress: House, 1987c:26). Finally, and perhaps most important (from our perspective), the hearings underscored the absence of research on the policy involvement activities of nonprofit groups: "no one knows what tax-exempt organizations are doing [in terms of political and lobbying activities]" (U.S. Congress: House, 1987b:7).

5. The concept of hegemony derives most directly from the work of Gramsci (Sassoon 1987). Contemporary Marxist-oriented authors such as Navarro (1980, 1986) and Elling (1986) have utilized this concept in their research on health and medicine. Elling (1986:112, 118) has defined the concept this way: "Hegemony encompasses the complex interlocking of political, social, and cultural relations of domination. . . . The success of a ruling class in establishing hegemony depends entirely on its ability to convince the [other] classes that its interests are those of society at large--that it defends the common sensibility and stands for a natural and proper social order." In this context, the idea of a "hegemonic corporate culture" (especially vis-a-vis professional societies) means that the interests and policy views of corporate entities are deeply entrenched and shared by many of the members and leaders of the professional organizations which participate in and help to shape national health policy directions and outcomes. As a result of the structural linkages which the corporate sector has constructed connecting it to many of the professional groups, it is both politically and culturally dominant within many of these organizations. That is, within many of the professional associations (as well as within the larger society), the powerful, hegemonic position of the corporate sector produces effects whereby the interests and policy views of the business community come to be viewed as rational, reasonable, and legitimate.

6. The term *weltanschauung* is derived from Mannheim (1936, 1972) and generally refers to the idea of a "world view" composed of intersecting values and ideas which view and support the existing social, economic, and political order as just, fair, rational, and even "natural" (Mannheim 1972, especially 33-84).

7. The resources available for improving the technical competence of occupational health and safety professionals have increased dramatically since the passage of the OSH Act. In fact, "some occupational health professionals joked that the acronym--OSHA--stood for 'our savior has arrived'" (Walsh 1987:61). By this, they meant that government-mandated action in the area of occupational health and safety issues would not only place more resources at their disposal, but also that the law would help to legitimate and enhance the status and opportunities of occupational health and safety professionals generally.

REFERENCES

AAOHN Journal. 1986. AAOHN Code of Ethics. 34(8):365.

_____. 1987a. Annual Report. 35(3):125-131.

_____. 1987b. AAOHN Officers/Directors. 35(10):Directory.

AAOHN News. 1987a. AAOHN Supporting Legislation. 7(4):1.

_____. 1987b. AAOHN Supports Senate Bill. 7(12):1.

Ahlberg, R. 1989. RE: Corporate Influence on Threshold Limit Values. *American Journal of Industrial Medicine* 15:233.

Aldrich, H. 1976. Resource Dependence and Interorganizational Relations. *Administration & Society* 7(4):419-453.

_____. 1979. *Organizations and Environments.* Englewood Cliffs, N.J.: Prentice Hall.

Alford, R. 1975. *Health Care Politics.* Chicago: University of Chicago Press.

American Industrial Hygiene Association Journal. 1987a. AIHA News . . . AIHA Public Positions: Procedure. 48(6):A-420.

_____. 1987b. Code of Ethics. 48(8):A-546.

_____. 1988. AIHA Organizational Members. 49(2):A-112-17.

American Journal of Public Health. 1985. 8415(PP):Compensation for and Prevention of Environmental Diseases. 75(3):302-305.

_____. 1987. 8607: Worker Notification of Adverse Health Findings. 77(1):103-104.

American Medical News. 1987a. M.D. Income is Steady, Liability Costs Up: Report. (February 13) 30(6):2, 17.

_____. 1987b. Candidates Will Be Elected at the AMA Annual Meeting, June 21-25 In Chicago. (June 5) 30(21):37.

_____. 1987c. Two Unopposed in Bids for Election to Top AMA Posts. (June 12) 30(22):17.

_____. 1988a. AMA Newsletter. (March 4) 31(9):8.

_____. 1988b. Business Briefs. (November 25) 31(44):14.

_____. 1988c. Dr. Davis, Next AMA President, Sets His Sights on Stressing Service Ethic. (May 27) 31(20):1, 20.

_____. 1988d. Candidates Running for AMA Offices. (June 3) 31(21):31-32.

Applied Industrial Hygiene. 1987. ACGIH Resolutions Ratified at the 1987 AIHC. 2(5):F-22, F-24.

Ashford, N. A. 1976. *Crisis in the Workplace: Occupational Disease and Injury.* Cambridge, Massachusetts: MIT Press.

Auerbach, J. S. 1976. *Unequal Justice: Lawyers and Social Change in America.* New York: Oxford University Press.

Bachrach, P. and M. S. Baratz. 1970. *Power and Poverty, Theory and Practice.* New York: Oxford University Press.

Badaracco J. L., Jr. 1985. *Loading the Dice.* Boston: Harvard Business School Press.

Balbus, I. D. 1971. The Concept of Interest in Pluralist and Marxian Analysis. *Politics and Society* 1(2):151-77.

Bayer, R. 1986. Notifying Workers at Risk: The Politics of the Right-to-Know. *American Journal of Public Health* 26(11):1352-1356.

Bazelon, D. L. 1977. Coping with Technology Through The Legal Process. *Cornell Law Review* 62:817-828.

_____. 1979. Risk and Responsibility. *Science* (July 20) 205:277-280.

Benson, J. K. 1975. The Interorganizational Network as a Political Economy. *Administrative Science Quarterly* 20(2):229-249.

Berlant, J. L. 1976. *Professions and Monopoly: A Study of Medicine in the United States and Great Britain.* Berkeley: University of California Press.

Berman, D. M. 1978. *Death on the Job.* New York: Monthly Review Press.

Bernstein, C. and B. Woodward. 1974. *All the President's Men.* New York: Simon and Schuster.

Bingham, R. D., B. W. Hawkins, J. P. Frendreis, and M. P. Le Blanc. 1981. *Professional Associations and Municipal Innovation.* Madison: University of Wisconsin Press.

Bodnar, E. M. 1988. Occupational Health Nurses Emerge as Future Corporate Care Managers. *Occupational Health and Safety* (April):21, 24.

Brannon, R. L. 1990. The Reorganization of the Nursing Labor Process: From Team to Primary Nursing. *International Journal of Health Services* 20(3):511-524.

Brickman, R., S. Jasanoff, and T. Ilgen. 1985. *Controlling Chemicals.* Ithaca: Cornell University Press.

Brint, S. 1984. New Class and Cumulative Trend Explanations of the Liberal Political Attitudes of Professionals. *American Journal of Sociology* 90:30-71.

_____. 1987. Classification Struggles: Reply to Lamont. *American Journal of Sociology* 92(6):1506-1509.

Brodeur, P. 1974. *Expendable Americans.* New York: The Viking Press.

Brown, E. R. 1979. *Rockefeller Medicine Men.* Berkeley: University of California Press.

Burnham, D. 1977. Agency Lists but Does Not Notify Workers Exposed to Carcinogens. *New York Times* (April 25):18.

Calavita, K. 1983. The Demise of the Occupational Safety and Health Administration. *Social Problems* 30(4):437-48.

Cannella, J. M. 1987. Special Communication--Occupational Physician Scholarship Fund. *Journal of Occupational Medicine* 29(2):151-152.

Carr-Saunders, A. M. and P. A. Wilson. 1933. *The Professions.* Oxford: Oxford University Press.

Castleman, B. I. and G. E. Ziem. 1988. Corporate Influence on Threshold Limit Values. *American Journal of Industrial Medicine* 13(5):531-559.

Cockburn, A. 1991. Ashes & Diamonds. *In These Times* (June 26-July 9):17.

Cockerham, W. C. 1986. *Medical Sociology.* Englewood Cliffs, N.J.: Prentice-Hall.

Cohen, R. E. 1989. Selecting His Targets With Care. *National Journal* (January 21):175.

Cohodas, N. 1987. Labor, Health Groups Push to Notify Workers of Hazards. *Congressional Quarterly Weekly Report* (February 28) 45(9):374-375.

Collins, R. 1979. *The Credential Society.* New York: Academic Press.

Congressional Record. 1985. Public Bills and Resolutions.(February 27):H816.

_____. 1986. Support Grows For Occupational Disease Notification Measure. (October 7):H9421-2.

_____. 1987. High-Risk Occupational Disease Notification and Prevention Act of 1987. (October 14):H8615-8671.

_____. 1988a. High-Risk Occupational Disease Notification and Prevention Act. (March 22):S2767-2788.

_____. 1988b. High-Risk Occupational Disease Notification and Prevention Act. (March 28):S3150-3181.

_____. 1988c. High-Risk Occupational Disease Notification and Prevention Act. (March 29):S3223-3234.

_____. 1989a. Introduction of the High-Risk Occupational Disease Notification and Prevention Act of 1989. (August 1):H4696-4698.

_____. 1989b. Introduction of Bills and Joint Resolutions. S. 582. (March 15):S2570.

_____. 1989c. High-Risk Occupational Disease Notification and Prevention Act. (March 15):S2673-2680.

_____. 1989d. Public Resolutions and Bills. H.R. 3067. (August 1):H4844.

_____. 1991a. Comprehensive Occupational Safety And Health Reform Act. (August 2):E2858-60.

_____. 1991b. Comprehensive Occupational Safety And Health Reform Act. (August 1):S11833-11845.

Coombes, P. 1989. EPCA: Shining Industry's Image. *Chemicalweek* (October 11):14.

Coye, M. J., M. D. Smith, and A. Mazzocchi. 1984. Occupational Health and Safety: Two Steps Forward, One Step Back. *Reforming Medicine*, eds. V. W. and R. Sidel, 79-106. New York: Pantheon.

Cralley, L. J. 1988. Industrial Hygiene is a Viable Profession. *American Industrial Hygiene Association Journal* 49(10):479-484.

de Kervasdoue, J. and V. G. Rodwin. 1984. Health Policy and the Expanding Role of the State: 1945-1980. *The End of an Illusion*, eds. J. de Kervasdoue, J. R. Kimberly, and V. G. Rodwin, 3-32. Berkeley: University of California Press.

Derber, C. 1982. *Professionals as Workers: Mental Labor in Advanced Capitalism*. Boston: G.K. Hall.

_____. 1983. Sponsorship and Control of Physicians. *Theory and Society* 12(5):561-601.

DiMaggio, P. J. and H. K. Anheier. 1990. The Sociology of Nonprofit Organizations and Sectors. *Annual Review of Sociology*, Vol.16, eds. W. R. Scott and J. Blake, 137-159. Palo Alto, Calif.: Annual Reviews, Inc.

Dingwall, R. and P. Lewis, eds. 1983. *The Sociology of the Professions*. New York: St. Martin's Press.

Domhoff, G. W. 1978. *The Powers That Be*. New York: Random House.

_____. 1983. *Who Rules America Now?*. Englewood Cliffs, N.J.: Prentice-Hall.

_____. 1987. Where Do Government Experts Come From? *Power Elites and Organizations*, eds. G. W. Domhoff and T. R. Dye, 189-200. Newbury Park, Calif.: Sage.

Donnelly, P. G. 1982. The Origins of the Occupational Safety and Health Act of 1970. *Social Problems* 30(1):11-25.

Durkheim, E. 1964. *The Division of Labor in Society*, 2nd ed. New York: Free Press.

Edelman, M. 1964. *The Symbolic Uses of Politics*. Chicago: University of Illinois Press.

_____. 1979. *Political Language: Words That Succeed and Policies That Fail*. New York: Academic Press.

_____. 1988. *Constructing The Political Spectacle*. Chicago: University of Chicago Press.

Ehrenreich, J. and B. Ehrenreich. 1977. The Professional-Managerial Class. *Radical America* 11:7-31.

Elling, R. H. 1986. *The Struggle for Workers' Health*. Farmingdale, N.Y.: Baywood Publishing Co., Inc.

Epstein, S. S. 1990. Losing the War Against Cancer: Who's to Blame and What to do About It. *International Journal of Health Services* 20(1):53-72.

Esping-Andersen, G. 1985. Power and Distributional Regimes. *Politics and Society* 14(2):223-256.

Farrar, A. 1987. President's Page. *American Industrial Hygiene Association Journal* 48(4):A-234, A-236.

Federal Election Commission. 1985-1986. Candidate Index of Supporting Documents (E), Bumpers, Dale. FEC Print Out. 1-24.

———. 1987-1988. Candidate Index of Supporting Documents (E), Hatch, Orrin G. FEC Print Out. 1-57.

———. 1987-88. Committee Index of Disclosure Documents (C), American Medical Political Action Committee (AMPAC). FEC Print Out. 1-2.

———. 1987-88. Independent Expenditures and Communication Costs. Independent Expenditure Index by Committee/Person Expending. AMPAC. FEC Print Out. July 9, 1989:29-31.

———. 1988. FEC Final Report on 1986 PAC Activity. (May 5):1-28.

———. 1988-89. AMPAC Itemized Disbursements January through December. FEC Microfilm Rolls: 88FEC/510, 88FEC/513, 88FEC/518, 88FEC/523, 88FEC/526, 88FEC/529, 88FEC/530, 88FEC/538, 88FEC/540, 88FEC/542, 88FEC/547, 88FEC/556, 88FEC/563, 88FEC/569, 89FEC/579.

Feinglass, J. and J. W. Salmon. 1990. Corporatization of Medicine: The Use of Medical Management Information Systems to Increase the Clinical Productivity of Physicians. *International Journal of Health Services* 20(2):233-252.

Feldstein, P. J. 1977. *Health Associations and the Demand for Legislation.* Cambridge, Massachusetts: Ballinger.

———. 1987. Policies of the American Medical Profession: Self-Interest or Public Interest? *Dominant Issues in Medical Sociology,* 2nd ed., ed. H. D. Schwartz, 549-588. New York: Random House.

Ford, R. L. 1988. *Work, Organization and Power.* Needham Heights, Massachusetts: Allyn and Bacon.

Freidson, E. 1970a. *Professional Dominance.* New York: Atherton Press.

———. 1970b. *Profession of Medicine.* New York: Harper and Row.

———. 1984. Are Professions Necessary? *The Authority of Experts,* ed. T. L. Haskell, 3-27. Bloomington: Indiana University Press.

———. 1985. The Reorganization of the Medical Profession. *Medical Care Review* 42(1):11-35.

———. 1986. *Professional Powers.* Chicago: University of Chicago Press.

———. 1989. *Medical Work in America.* New Haven: Yale University Press.

Fulton, J. F., ed. 1958. Henry Sigerist Memorial Issue. *Journal of the History of Medicine and Allied Sciences* Vol. XIII(2):125-250.

Gais, T. L., M. A. Peterson, and J. L. Walker. 1984. Interest Groups, Iron Triangles and Representative Institutions in American National Government. *British Journal of Political Science* 14(3):161-185.

Galaskiewicz, J. 1985. Interorganizational Relations. *Annual Review of Sociology*, Vol. 11, eds. R. H. Turner and J.F. Short, Jr., 281-304. Palo Alto, Calif.: Annual Reviews, Inc.

Gamson, W. 1975. *The Strategy of Social Protest*. Homewood, Illinois: Dorsey Press.

Garceau, O. 1941. *The Political Life of the American Medical Association*. Cambridge: Harvard University Press.

Gilb, C. L. 1966. *Hidden Hierarchies: The Professions and Government*. New York: Harper and Row.

Glaser, B. G. and A. L. Strauss. 1967. *The Discovery of Grounded Theory: Strategies for Qualitative Research*. New York: Aldine.

Goode, W. J. 1960. Encroachment, Charlatanism, and the Emerging Professions: Psychology, Medicine and Sociology. *American Sociological Review* 25:902-14.

Gouldner, A. W. 1959. Organizational Analysis. *Sociology Today*, eds. R. K. Merton, L. Broom and L. S. Cottrell, 400-428. New York: Basic Books.

Granovetter, M. 1985. Economic Action and Social Structure: The Problem of Embeddedness. *American Journal of Sociology* 91:481-510.

Hall, R. H. 1986. *Dimensions of Work*. Beverly Hills: Sage.

Halliday, T. C. 1987. *Beyond Monopoly*. Chicago: University of Chicago Press.

Hargrove, B. 1986. *The Emerging New Class: Implications for Church and Society*. New York: Pilgrim Press.

Harvey, M. 1991. 100 Million Working Stiffs Disappear. *Utne Reader* (May/June):20-23.

Haskell, T. L. 1984. Professionalism *versus* Capitalism:R. H. Tawney, E. Durkheim, and C. S. Pierce on the Distinterestedness of Professional Communities. *The Authority of Experts*, ed. T. L. Haskell, 180-225. Bloomington: Indiana University Press.

Health Letter. 1991. Outrage of the Month. Vol. 7 (No.6, June):12.

Hodson, R. and R. L. Kaufman. 1982. Economic Dualism: A Critical Review. *American Sociological Review* 47:727-39.

Hunter, J. D. 1980. The New Class and the Evangelicals. *Review of Religious Research* 22:155-169.

Illich, I. 1976. The Need-Makers. *The Professions and Public Policy*, eds. P. Slayton and M. J. Trebilcock, 341-346. Toronto: University of Toronto Press.

Jacobs, J. A. 1986. *Association Law Handbook*. Washington, D.C.: The Bureau of National Affairs.

Jenkins, J. C. 1983. Resource Mobilization Theory and the Study of Social Movements. *Annual Review of Sociology*, Vol. 9, eds. R. H. Turner and J. F. Short, 527-553. Palo Alto, Calif.: Annual Reviews, Inc.

Johnson, W. M. and W. D. Parnes. 1979. Beta-naphthylamine and Benzidine: Identification of Groups at High Risk of Bladder Cancer. *Annals of the New York Academy of Sciences* 329:277-284.

Journal of the American Medical Association. 1988. AMA Insights. 259(16):2371.

Journal of Occupational Medicine. 1976. Code of Ethical Conduct For Physicians Providing Occupational Medical Services. 18(8): Cover Page.

_____. 1985. Association Affairs. 27(12):921-924.

_____. 1987. American Occupational Medical Association Officers, Directors. 29(12):991.

Judkins, B. M. 1986. *We Offer Ourselves as Evidence*. New York: Greenwood Press.

Karr, A. R. 1987. House Plans Vote On Bill for Notice Of Work Hazards. *Wall Street Journal* (October 14):59.

Keiser, K. R. and W. Jones, Jr. 1986. Do the American Medical Association's Campaign Contributions Influence Health Care Legislation? *Medical Care* 24(8):761-766.

Kelman, S. 1981. *Regulating America, Regulating Sweden: A Comparative Study of Occupational Safety and Health Policy*. Cambridge, Massachusetts: MIT Press.

Knoke, D. and J. H. Kuklinski. 1982. *Network Analysis*. Beverly Hills: Sage.

Knudsen, P. L. 1987. Risk Notification Legislation Passed by House. *Congressional Quarterly Weekly Report* (October 17) 45(2):2513-2515.

Koek, K. E., S. B. Martin, and A. Novallo, eds. 1988. *Encyclopedia of Associations*, 23rd ed., Vol. I, Parts I and II. Detroit: Gale Research.

Korpi, W. 1983. *The Democratic Class Struggle*. London: Routledge and Kegan Paul.

Kronenfeld, J. J. and M. L. Whicker. 1984. *U.S. National Health Policy*. New York: Praeger.

Kusnetz, H. L. 1986a. President's Page. *American Industrial Hygiene Association Journal* 47(2):A-72.

_____. 1986b. President's Page. *American Industrial Hygiene Association Journal* 47(3):A-136.

Kwik, P. 1991. Tragic Poultry Fire Emphasizes the Urgency of Southern Organizing. *Labor Notes* (October):16.

154   References

Lamont, M. 1987. Cultural Capital and the Liberal Political Attitudes of Professionals: Comment on Brint. *American Journal of Sociology* 92(6):1501-1505.

Larson, M. 1977. *The Rise of Professionalism.* Berkeley: University of California Press.

Laumann, E. O. and D. Knoke. 1987. *The Organizational State: Social Choice in National Policy Domains.* Madison: University of Wisconsin Press.

Lee, J. 1987. A Message From The Chair. *Applied Industrial Hygiene* 2(1):F-7-F-8.

LeRoy, G. 1991. Profitable Low Wage Southern Plants to Close: Procter-Silex says Mexico is Even Cheaper. *Labor Notes* (July):7.

Levin, D. P. 1991. Detroit's Assault on Mileage Bill. *New York Times* (May 11):35 & 37.

Levine, S. and A.M. Lilienfeld. 1987. Introduction. *Epidemiology and Health Policy*, eds. S. Levine and A. M. Lilienfeld, 1-14. New York: Tavistock.

Leviton, L., G. Marsh, E. Talbot, D. Pavlock, and C. Callahan. 1991. Drake Chemical Workers' Health Registry: Coping with Community Tension over Toxic Exposures. *American Journal of Public Health* 81(6):689-693.

Lowi, T. J. 1964. American Business, Public Policy, Case-Studies, and Political Theory. *World Politics* Vol.XVI(4):677-715.

Lynn, F. M. 1986. The Interplay of Science and Values in Assessing and Regulating Environmental Risks. *Science, Technology, and Human Values* 11(2):40-50.

Macy, M. 1988. New-Class Dissent Among Social-Cultural Specialists: The Effects of Occupational Self-Direction and Location in the Public Sector. *Sociological Forum* 3:325-356.

Mannheim, K. 1936. *Ideology and Utopia.* New York: Harcourt, Brace and World, Inc.

_____. 1972. *Essays on the Sociology of Knowledge*, ed. P. Kecskemeti. London: Routledge and Kegan Paul.

Marder, W. D., D. W. Emmons, P. R. Kletke, and R. J. Willke. 1988. Physician Employment Patterns: Challenging Conventional Wisdom. *Health Affairs* (Winter):137-145.

Marmor, T. R. 1973. *The Politics of Medicare.* Chicago:Aldine.

Marsden, P. V. 1990. Network Data and Measurement. *Annual Review of Sociology*, Vol. 16, eds. W. R. Scott and J.Blake, 435-463. Palo Alto, Calif.: Annual Reviews, Inc.

Marshall, C. and G. B. Rossman. 1989. *Designing Qualitative Research.* Newbury Park, Calif.: Sage.

Matlack, C. 1987. Worker Warnings Switches to Fast Track. *National Journal* (April 4) 19(4):832-833.

McAdams, J. 1987. Testing the Theory of the New Class. *Sociological Quarterly* 28:23-49.

McCaffrey, D. P. 1982. *OSHA and the Politics of Health Regulation*. New York: Plenum Press.

McCarthy, J. D. and M. N. Zald. 1977. Resource Mobilization and Social Movements. *American Journal of Sociology* 82(6):1212-1241.

McKinlay, J. B. 1982. Toward the Proletarianization of Physicians. *Professionals as Workers: Mental Labor in Advanced Capitalism*, ed. C. Derber, 37-62. Boston: G. K. Hall.

McKinlay, J. B. and J. Arches. 1985. Towards the Proletarianization of Physicians. *International Journal of Health Services* 15(2):161-195.

McMichael, P. 1990. Incorporating Comparisons Within A World-Historical Perspective: An Alternative Comparative Method. *American Sociological Review* 55:385-397.

Mechanic, D. 1972. *Public Expectations and Health Care*. New York: Wiley-Interscience.

Mendeloff, J. M. 1988. *The Dilemma of Toxic Substance Regulation*. Cambridge, Massachusetts: MIT Press.

Milio, N. 1981. *Promoting Health Through Public Policy*. Philadelphia: F. A. Davis Co.

_____. 1988. The Profitization of Health Promotion. *International Journal of Health Services* 18(4):573-585.

Miller, D. K. 1972. Scientific Societies and Public Responsibilities. *Annals of the New York Academy of Sciences* 196(4):247-255.

Mills, C. W. 1956. *The Power Elite*. New York: Oxford University Press.

Mintz, B. W. 1984. *OSHA, History, Law, and Policy*. Washington, D.C.: The Bureau of National Affairs.

Mizruchi, M. 1987. Why Do Corporations Stick Together? *Power Elites and Organizations*, eds. G. W. Domhoff and T. R. Dye, 204-218. Beverly Hills: Sage.

Morehouse, M. 1988a. Senate Battling Over Risk-Notification Bill. *Congressional Quarterly Weekly Report* (March 26) 46(13):781-782.

_____. 1988b. Risk Notification Measure Derailed by GOP Filibuster. *Congressional Quarterly Weekly Report* (April 2) 46(14):842.

The Nation's Health. 1986. Worker Notification of Adverse Health Findings. (August):8.

_____. 1987. Bill to Require Notifying Workers of Job Hazards is Before Congress. (September):1, 32.

_____. 1988a. *Explanations* 15 House Votes. (February):10-13.

_____. 1988b. GOP Filibuster Blocks Worker Risk Notification. (May-June):5.

Navarro, V. 1976. *Medicine Under Capitalism*. New York: Prodist.

_____. 1980. Work, Ideology, and Science. *Social Science and Medicine* 14C:191-295.

_____. 1982. The Crisis of the International Capitalist Order and its Implications for the Welfare State. *International Journal of Health Services* 12(2):169-189.

_____. 1983. Radicalism, Marxism, and Medicine. *International Journal of Health Services* 13(2):179-202.

_____. 1984. The Determinants of Health Policy, A Case Study: Regulating Safety and Health at the Workplace in Sweden. *Journal of Health Politics, Policy, and Law* 9(1):137-156.

_____. 1985. U.S. Marxist Scholarship in the Analysis of Health and Medicine. *International Journal of Health Services* 15(4):525-545.

_____. 1986. *Crisis, Health, and Medicine*. New York: Tavistock.

_____. 1991. Production and the Welfare State: The Political Context of Reforms. *International Journal of Health Services* 21(4):585-614.

Neustadtl, A. 1990. Interest-Group PACmanship: An Analysis of Campaign Contributions, Issue Visibility, and Legislative Impact. *Social Forces* 69:549-564.

New York Times. 1984. Keeping Ill Workers in Ignorance. (November 2):A26.

Noble, C. 1986. *The Rise and Fall of OSHA*. Philadelphia: Temple University Press.

Nothstein, G. Z. 1981. *The Law of Occupational Safety and Health*. New York: The Free Press.

Occupational Safety and Health Reporter. 1987a. Coalition Solicits Opposition on Hill to High Risk Legislation. (April 8):1186-7.

_____. 1987b. Proposed High Risk Bill Would Create Enormous Liabilities, Tyson Says. (September 23):748-9.

_____. 1988. Effort To Warn Beryllium Workers Of Possible Disease Risk Planned By DOE. (July 13):501-2.

_____. 1989. Concern for Job Safety & Health Issues Seen Rising in Next Decade, Conference Told. (September 27):755-56.

Omang, J. 1981. Millions Not Told of Job Health Perils. *Washington Post* (August 24):A1, A5.

Oppenheimer, M. 1985. *White Collar Politics*. New York: Monthly Review Press.

Page, J. A. and M. W. O'Brien. 1973. *Bitter Wages*. New York: Grossman.

Palmer, D., R. Friedland, and J. V. Singh. 1986. The Ties That Bind: Organizational And Class Bases Of Stability in a Corporate Interlock Network. *American Sociological Review* 15(6):781-796.

Parsons, T. 1939. The Professions and Social Structure. *Social Forces* 17(4):457-467.

Perrow, C. 1986. *Complex Organizations*, 3rd ed., New York: Random House.

Perrucci, R., R. M. Anderson, D. E. Schendel, and L. E. Trachtman. 1980. Whistle-Blowing:Professionals'Resistanceto OrganizationalAuthority. *Social Problems* 28(2):149-164.

Perrucci, R. and B. L. Lewis. 1989. Interorganizational Relations and Community Influence Structure: A Replication and Extension. *The Sociological Quarterly* 30(2):205-223.

Peters, B. G. 1986. *American Public Policy*. Chatham, N.J.: Chatham House Publishers, Inc.

Peterson, M. A. and J. L. Walker. 1986. Interest Group Responses to Partisan Change: The Impact of the Reagan Administration upon the National Interest Group System. *Interest Group Politics*, eds. A. J. Cigler and B. A. Loomis, 162-182. Washington, D.C.: Congressional Quarterly, Inc.

Pfeffer, J. 1982. *Organizations and Organizational Theory*. Boston: Pitman Publishing Co.

Pfeffer, J. and G. R. Salancik. 1978. *The External Control of Organizations: A Resource Dependence Perspective*. New York: Harper and Row.

Professional Safety. 1985. OSHA News. 30(11):8-9.

_____. 1986. The First 75 Years. 31(10):10, i-17.

_____. 1987a. Annual Report. 32(10):5, 1-12.

_____. 1987b. Upfront. 32(10):1.

_____. 1988. Upfront. 33(9):1.

_____. 1989a. Society Update. 34(2):29.

_____. 1989b. OSHA News. 34(2):8, 33.

Ragin, C. C. 1987. *The Comparative Method*. Berkeley: University of California Press.

Ratcliffe, J. and L. Wallack. 1985-86. Primary Prevention in Public Health: An Analysis of Basic Assumptions. *International Quarterly of Health Education* 6(3):215-39.

Ratcliffe, J., L. Wallack, F. Fagnani, and V. G. Rodkin. 1984. Perspectives on Prevention: Health Promotion vs. Health Protection. *The End of an Illusion*, eds. J. de Kervasdoue, J. R. Kimberly, and V. G. Rodwin, 56-84. Berkeley: University of California Press.

Renaud, M. 1975. On the Structural Constraints to State Intervention in Health. *International Journal of Health Services* 5(4):559-571.

Roback, G., L. Randolph, B. Seidman, and D. Mead. 1987. *Physician Characteristics and Distribution in the U.S.* Chicago: American Medical Association.

Robinson, J. C. and D. G. Paxton. 1991. OSHA's Four Inconsistent Carcinogen Policies. *American Journal of Public Health* 81(6):775-780.

Rohrer, J. E. 1987. The Political Development of the Hill-Burton Program: A Case Study in Distributive Policy. *Journal of Health Politics, Policy and Law* 12(1):137-52.

Rosen, G. 1948. Approaches to a Concept of Social Medicine. A Historical Survey. *The Milbank Memorial Fund Quarterly* Vol. XXVI(1):7-21.

————. 1974. *From Medical Police to Social Medicine: Essays on the History of Health Care.* New York: Science History Publications.

Ross, D. M. 1988. Professionalism and Ethics. *Applied Industrial Hygiene* 3(8):F-17-F-19.

Rothman, R. 1987. *Working--Sociological Perspectives.* Englewood Cliffs, N.J.: Prentice-Hall.

Ruttenberg, R. and M. Powers. 1986. Economics of Notification and Medical Screening for High-Risk Workers. *Journal of Occupational Medicine* 28(8):757-64.

Saffiotti, U. and J. K. Wagoner, eds. 1976. Occupational Carcinogenesis. *Annals of the New York Academy of Sciences* 271:1-516.

Sassoon, A. S. 1987. *Gramsci's Politics.* Minneapolis: University of Minnesota Press.

Schlozman, K. L. and J. T. Tierney. 1986. *Organized Interests and American Democracy.* New York: Harper and Row.

Schulte, P. A. and K. Ringen. 1984. Notification of Workers at High Risk: An Emerging Public Health Problem. *American Journal of Public Health* 75(5):485-91.

Schulte, P. A., K. Ringen, E. B. Altekruse, W. H. Gullen, K. Davidson, S. Anderson, and M. Patton. 1985. Notification of a Cohort of Workers at Risk of Bladder Cancer. *Journal of Occupational Medicine* 27(1):19-28.

Selikoff, I. J. 1976. Lung Cancer and Mesothelioma During Prospective Surveillance of 1249 Asbestos Insulation Workers: 1963-1974. *Annals of the New York Academy of Sciences* 271(VIII):448-455.

Selikoff, I. J. and E. C. Hammond, eds. 1979. Health Hazards of Asbestos Exposure. *Annals of the New York Academy of Sciences* 330:1-800.

Shadish, W. R. 1987. Program Micro- and Macrotheories: A Guide for Social Change. *Using Program Theory in Evaluation,* ed. L. Bickman, 93-108. San Francisco: Jossey-Bass.

Shaffir, W. B., R. A. Stebbins, and A. Turowetz. 1980. *Fieldwork Experience.* New York: St. Martin's Press.

Shaw, G. B. 1954. *The Doctor's Dilemma.* Baltimore: Penguin Books.

Sheehan, J. J. 1982. Cost Benefit Analysis: A Technique Gone Awry. *Legal and Ethical Dilemmas In Occupational Health*, eds. J. S. Lee and W. N. Rom, 51-76. Ann Arbor: Ann Arbor Science Publishers.

Sidel, V. and R. Sidel, eds. 1984. *Reforming Medicine*. New York: Pantheon Books.

Sigerist, H. E. 1941. *Medicine and Human Welfare*. New Haven: Yale University Press.

_____. 1943. *Civilization and Disease*. Ithaca: Cornell University Press.

Silver, G. A. 1984. Social Medicine and Social Policy. *The Yale Journal of Biology and Medicine* 57(6):851-864.

Skocpol, T. 1984. Emerging Agendas and Recurrent Strategies in Historical Sociology. *Vision and Method in Historical Sociology*, ed. T. Skocpol, 356-391. Cambridge: Cambridge University Press.

Starr, P. 1982. *The Social Transformation of American Medicine*. New York: Basic Books.

Stevens, R. 1971. *American Medicine and the Public Interest*. New Haven: Yale University Press.

Swankin, D. A. Washington Letter. 1988. *American Industrial Hygiene Association Journal* 49(1):A-8.

_____. 1989. Washington Report. *Professional Safety* 34(2):5.

Szasz, A. 1984. Industrial Resistance to Occupational Safety and Health Legislation: 1971-1981. *Social Problems* 32(2):103-116.

_____. 1986. The Reversal of Federal Policy Toward Worker Safety. *Science & Society* Vol. L(1):25-51.

Tasini, J. 1990. Point of View: Where Was Dan? *Solidarity* (November):28.

Taylor, R. and A. Rieger. 1984. Rudolf Virchow on the Typhus Epidemic in Upper Silesia: An Introduction and Translation. *Sociology of Health and Illness* 6(2):201-217.

Terris, M. 1987. Redefining the Public Health Agenda. *Journal of Public Health Policy* (Summer):151-163.

Tesh, S. 1988. *Hidden Arguments: Political Ideology and Disease Prevention Policy*. New Brunswick: Rutgers University Press.

Thompson, F. J. 1981. *Health Policy and the Bureaucracy*. Cambridge, Massachusetts: MIT Press.

Thompson, H. S. 1988. *Generation of Swine*. New York: Summitt.

Tierney, J. T. 1987. Organized Interests in Health Politics and Policy-Making. *Medical Care Review* 44(1):89-118.

Tillett S., K. Ringen, P. Schulte, V. McDougall, K. Miller, and S. Samuels. 1986. Interventions in High-Risk Occupational Cohorts: A Cross-Sectional Demonstration Project. *Journal of Occupational Medicine* 28(8):719-27.

Titmuss, R. 1959. *Essays on 'The Welfare State'*. New Haven: Yale University Press.

Truman, D. B. 1962. *The Governmental Process: Political Interests and Public Opinion*. New York: Alfred A. Knopf.

U.S. Congress: House Committee on Education and Labor. Subcommittee on Labor. 1974. *Occupational Safety and Health Act of 1970, (Oversight and Proposed Amendments)*. 94th Cong. 2nd sess. Washington, D.C.: Government Printing Office.

_____. Committee on Government Operations. Subcommittee on Manpower and Housing. 1975. *Safety in the Federal Workplace*. 94th Cong., 1st sess. Washington, D.C.: Government Printing Office.

_____. Committee on Government Operations. Subcommittee on Manpower and Housing. 1976. *Control of Toxic Substances in the Workplace*. 94th Cong., 2nd sess. Washington, D.C.: Government Printing Office.

_____. Committee on Education and Labor. Subcommittee on Labor Standards. 1982. *Occupational Health Hazards Compensation Act of 1982*. 97th Cong., 2nd sess. Washington, D.C.: Government Printing Office.

_____. Committee on Education and Labor. Subcommittee on Labor Standards. 1983. *Hearings on the Occupational Disease Compensation Act of 1983*. 98th Cong., 1st sess. Washington, D.C.: Government Printing Office.

_____. Committee on Education and Labor. Subcommittee on Health and Safety and the Subcommittee on Labor Standards. 1985. *The High Risk Occupational Disease Notification and Prevention Act of 1985*. 99th Cong., 1st and 2nd sessions. serial no. 99-117. Washington, D.C.: Government Printing Office.

_____. Committee on Education and Labor. Subcommittee on Health and Safety. 1987a. *High Risk Occupational Disease Notification and Prevention Act of 1987*. 100th Cong., 1st sess. serial no. 100-22. Washington, D.C.: Government Printing Office.

_____. Committee on Ways and Means. Subcommittee on Oversight. 1987b. *Lobbying and Political Activities of Tax-Exempt Organizations*. 100th Cong., 1st sess. serial no. 100-15. Washington, D.C.: Government Printing Office.

_____. Committee on Ways and Means. Subcommittee on Oversight. 1987c. *Unrelated Business Income Tax*. 100th Cong., 1st sess. serial no. 100-26. Washington, D.C.: Government Printing Office.

_____. Committee on Ways and Means. Subcommittee on Oversight. 1987d. *Lobbying and Political Activities of Tax-Exempt Organizations*. Report and Recommendations Committee Print, WMPC:100-12. 100th Cong., 1st sess. Washington, D.C.: Government Printing Office.

_____. Committee on Education and Labor. Subcommittee on Health and Safety. 1989. *General Oversight Hearing On The National Institute For Occupational Safety and Health (NIOSH)*. 101st Cong., 1st sess. serial no. 101-12. Washington, D.C.: Government Printing Office.

_____. Subcommittee on Health and Safety. 1985-88. Files of the Subcommittee regarding H.R. 1309 and H.R. 162. Washington, D.C.: Longworth House Office Building.

U.S. Congress: Office of Technology Assessment. 1985. *Preventing Illness and Injury in the Workplace*. Pub. No. OTA-H-256. Washington, D.C.: Government Printing Office.

U.S. Congress: Senate. Committee on Labor and Public Welfare. Subcommittee on Labor. 1969. *Occupational Safety and Health Act of 1970*. 91st Cong., 1st and 2nd sessions. Washington, D.C.: Government Printing Office.

_____. Committee on Human Resources. Subcommittee on Labor. 1977. *Monitoring of Industrial Workers Exposed to Carcinogens, 1977*. 95th Cong., 1st sess. Washington, D.C.: Government Printing Office.

_____. Committee on Labor and Human Resources. 1986. *Federal Incentives for State Health Care Professional Liability Reform Act of 1985*. 99th Cong., 2nd sess. Washington, D.C.: Government Printing Office.

_____. Committee on Labor and Human Resources. Subcommittee on Labor. 1987a. *High Risk Occupational Disease Notification and Prevention Act of 1987*. 100th Congress, 1st sess. Washington, D.C.: Government Printing Office.

_____. Committee on Labor and Human Resources. 1987b. *The High Risk Occupational Disease Notification And Prevention Act*. Report together with Minority Views, # 100-166. 100th Cong., 1st sess. Washington, D.C.: Government Printing Office.

_____. Committee On Small Business. 1987c. *The Impact On Small Business Of Legislation Requiring Notification To Workers Who Are At Risk Of Occupational Disease*. 100th Cong., 1st sess. S. Hrg. 100-149. Washington, D.C.: Government Printing Office.

_____. Subcommittee on Labor. 1986-88. Files of the Subcommittee regarding S. 79. Washington, D.C.: Senate Hart Office Building.

U.S. Department of the Treasury, Internal Revenue Service. 1989. *Internal Revenue Manual 7751, Exempt Organizations Handbook* (manual transmittal Sept. 12, 1989: 7751-88). pp. 7751-27-7751-119. Washington D.C.: Government Printing Office.

Useem, M. 1978. The Inner Group of the American Capitalist Class. *Social Problems* 25:225-240

_____. 1984. *The Inner Circle*. New York: Oxford University Press.

Ventura, M. 1991. Someone is Stealing Your Life. *Utne Reader* (July/August):78-80.

Victor, K. 1988. Step Under My Umbrella. *National Journal* 20(17):1063-1067.

Vogel, D. 1980. The Inadequacy of Contemporary Opposition to Business. *Daedalus* (Summer):47-58.

_____. 1983. The Power of Business: A Re-appraisal. *British Journal of Political Science* 13:19-43.

Waitzkin, H. 1983. *The Second Sickness*. New York: Free Press.

Waldo, D. 1973. Epilogue: Public Service Professional Associations in Context of Socio-Political Transition. *Public Service Professional Associations and the Public Interest*, ed. D. L. Bowen, 295-308. Philadelphia: American Academy of Political and Social Science.

Wallace, M. E. and B. A. Rubin. 1986. Capitalist Resistance to the Organization of Labor Before the New Deal: Why? How? Success? *American Sociological Review* 51:147-167.

Wallerstein, I. 1979. *The Capitalist World-Economy*. Cambridge: Cambridge University Press.

Wall Street Journal. 1988a. Xerox to Redeem Shares That It Issued for Crum & Forster. (February 3):31.

_____. 1988b. Xerox Corp. Sets Pact For Chemical Cleanup. (April 26):48.

_____. 1989. Xerox Settled Suits Over Chemical Leak in $4.75 Million Pact. (March 14):B5.

Walsh, D. C. 1987. *Corporate Physicians*. New Haven: Yale University Press.

Walters, V. 1982. Company Doctors' Perceptions of and Responses to Conflicting Pressures from Labor and Management. *Social Problems* 30(1):1-12.

_____. 1985. The Politics of Occupational Health and Safety: Interviews with Workers' Health and Safety Representatives and Company Doctors. *Canadian Review of Sociology and Anthropology* 22(1):57-79.

Webster, G. D. 1983. What Are the Lobbying Limits on 501(c)(6) And 501(c)(3) Groups? *Association Management* 35(2):39-41.

_____. 1985. Aspects of Association Lobbying. *Association Management* 37(11):53-54.

Weiser, B. 1989. Forging a 'Covenant of Silence.' *Washington Post* (March 13):1, A8.

Whitt, J. A. 1979. Toward a Class-Dialectical Model of Power: An Empirical Assessment of Three Competing Models of Political Power. *American Sociological Review* 44:81-100.

_____. 1982. *Urban Elites and Mass Transportation*. Princeton: Princeton University Press.

Wilensky, H. L. 1964. The Professionalization of Everyone? *American Journal of Sociology* 70:137-158.

Wilson, L. G., ed. 1978. George Rosen Memorial Issue. *Journal of the History of Medicine and Allied Sciences* Vol. XXXIII(3):244-313.

Wright, J. W. 1988. *The American Almanac of Jobs and Salaries.* New York: Avon Books.

Yin, R. K. 1984. *Case Study Research: Design and Methods.*Beverly Hills: Sage.

Zeitz, G. 1980. Interorganizational Dialectics. *Administrative Science Quarterly* 25(1):72-88.

Zey-Ferrell, M. and M. Aiken. 1981. Introduction to Critiques of Dominant Perspectives. *Complex Organizations: Critical Perspectives*, eds. M. Zey-Ferrell and M. Aiken, 1-21. Glenview, Illinois: Scott, Foresman and Co.

Ziem, G. E. and B. Castleman. 1989. Threshold Limit Values: Historical Perspectives and Current Practice. *Journal of Occupational Medicine* 31(11):910-918.

INDEX

About the Author

EARL WYSONG is Assistant Professor of Sociology at Indiana University at Kokomo. His earlier research has appeared in *Policy Studies Review* and, with Robert Perrucci, in the edited collection *Research and Politics in Society*.